Staring Down the Tiger

Staring Down the Tiger

STORIES OF HMONG AMERICAN WOMEN

Edited by Pa Der Vang

MINNESOTA
HISTORICAL
SOCIETY PRESS

mnhspress.org

The Minnesota Historical Society Press is a member of the Association of University Presses.

Manufactured in the United States of America

10 9 8 7 6 5 4 3 2 1

♾ The paper used in this publication meets the minimum requirements of the American National Standard for Information Sciences—Permanence for Printed Library Materials, ANSI Z39.48–1984.

International Standard Book Number
ISBN: 978-1-68134-150-7 (paper)
ISBN: 978-1-68134-153-8 (e-book)

Library of Congress Cataloging-in-Publication Data

Names: Vang, Pa Der, 1975– editor.
Title: Staring down the tiger : stories of Hmong American women / edited by Pa Der Vang.
Description: Saint Paul : Minnesota Historical Society Press, 2020. | Summary: "Hmong American women reclaim the phrase tsov tom or 'tiger bite,' showing in prose and poetry that they are strong enough and brave enough to stare down the tiger. Contributors celebrate the power of bonds between daughter and mother, sister and sister, and grandmother and granddaughter. These writers bring life and character to the challenges of maintaining identity, navigating changes in gender roles, transitioning to American culture, and breaking through cultural barriers." —Provided by publisher.
Identifiers: LCCN 2019047362 | ISBN 9781681341507 (paperback) | ISBN 9781681341538 (ebook)
Subjects: LCSH: American literature—Hmong American authors. | American literature—Women authors. | Hmong American women—Literary collections.
Classification: LCC PS508.H63 S73 2020 | DDC 810,8/0928708995972—dc23
LC record available at https://lccn.loc.gov/2019047362

This and other Minnesota Historical Society Press books are available from popular e-book vendors.

Hnub Tshiab: A New Day!
Valuing Women. Cultivating Leaders. Changing Lives.
This book is dedicated to Hmong women and girls.

Contents

Acknowledgments

Thank you to our supporters who made this book possible. We want to thank Wells Fargo for the initial funding that allowed us to begin this book. Thank you to MayKao Fredericks for believing in us and for always supporting Hmong women writers. Thank you to Kimberly Nightingale for your consultation and initial editing of the book and to the Minnesota Museum of American Art for opening your doors during our initial readings of selected works from this anthology. Thank you MaiThao Xiong, Ying Lee, and May Lee-Yang for your assistance in reviewing the first round of submissions for this book. Thank you to Ann Regan for believing in Hmong women. Finally, thank you to the Hmong women, mothers, grandmothers, aunts, daughters, and sisters in our lives whose stories form the basis for this book.

Preface

Pa Der Vang

It is that act of speech, of "talking back," that is no mere
gesture of empty words, that is the expression of our
movement from object to subject—the liberated voice.

—bell hooks, *Talking Back:*
Thinking Feminist, Thinking Black

Growing up, I was always curious about the role of Hmong
women in Hmong history. After seeing the movie *Mulan* as a
child, I thought maybe Hmong women also took part in their
journey from historical wars to America. After learning that
Hmong came from China, a part of me wanted to believe that
Mulan was Hmong, especially since this was my first time seeing
an American cartoon depicting an Asian female lead character.
I searched hard for stories about Hmong women in warrior or
leadership roles, but found none that had been documented. I
heard about Shwj Mim Mos, the Hmong Mulan, from stories
shared by Hmong women during community gatherings, but
no further details were provided about who she was, where she
came from, how she became this mythical character, what her
life was like, how she felt about her experience, what struggles
she endured. No one really knew. Hers was a story that was rarely
told. However, Shwj Mim Mos's existence, although in the shadows of men, gave evidence to girls that Hmong women were possibly warriors, too. Few people have heard about Shwj Mim Mos
since stories about Hmong women leaders are often left untold
in lieu of stories about Hmong men leaders.

I searched on the internet for Shwj Mim Mos and terms like
"Hmong Mulan," "Hmong women warriors," "historical Hmong

women leaders." I came upon a picture of nurse Choua Thao, who is often featured as an influential Hmong woman during the Vietnam War.[1] This picture was evidence to me that Hmong women played a very important role in our history during the war, yet it was difficult to find stories about other Hmong women beyond highlights about leaders like KaYing Yang, Bo Thao, Senator Mee Moua, MayKao Hang, Gaoly Yang, and Sy Vang Mouacheupao. Forgive me if I don't name all the women leaders, for it is very important in the Hmong culture to receive the appropriate recognition, an honor and privilege rarely given to Hmong women. The search for Hmong women leaders often landed me at the Minnesota Historical Society's "Hmong Women in Minnesota Timeline," which starts in 1975 and lists all of these names and more.

I was curious about the personal stories of Hmong women not only since their arrival in America but also in their journeys from Laos. They didn't have to be famous people or community leaders or involved in the military. Bringing their families from Laos to the United States involved some type of leadership, fortitude, and resilience, yet these stories were difficult to find. Creating a new life in a foreign land, raising children when you don't speak the language or understand the culture, earning a living and working for an employer who doesn't speak your language nor understand your culture, navigating changes in your relationships because the definitions of your role have drastically changed—all these responsibilities require courage, nimbleness, and discernment. It felt like Hmong women were just the objects in a story, objects whose agency and leadership were often ignored or dismissed by the larger narrative. My questions were: How did the women feel? What were their struggles? What did they think about? What were their worries? How did they endure and toil and survive such a difficult time? How did they do it?

---

1. Choua Thao resides in San Jose, California. She immigrated to the United States in April 1975, immediately following the end of the Vietnam War. She served as a nurse for the American Sam Thong Hospital at the age of twenty-two.

What was their thought process? I could not find answers in the literature. These stories about Hmong women were absent.

I wanted to bring life to the women, to honor them as the subjects in their own stories. Women have agency, yet they were portrayed as the objects in narratives about Hmong. I wanted to provide another platform to curate Hmong women's movement from object to subject.[2]

This book is the second publication in a project to share stories about Hmong women in America. An annual board retreat of Hnub Tshiab (pronounced *Hnoo Chia*): Hmong Women Achieving Together in 2015 served as a springboard for this book. We wanted to curate stories of Hmong women's leadership. We wanted to make available stories of Hmong women leaders for our Hmong boys and girls to consume. We recognized that Hmong women's stories are often absent in today's literature, especially in narratives about Hmong refugees in which the soldiers' stories are most valued. The first book, *Hmong Women Write Now: An Anthology of Creative Writing and Visual Artwork by Hmong Women and Girls,* was published in 2011 and edited by May Lee-Yang and Saymoukda Vongsay. This second book continues this work with a similar focus on collecting Hmong women's narratives. These stories have often been silenced throughout our long history. *Staring Down the Tiger* provides a platform for these stories to come to life. We are privileged to share these stories with the world.

---

2. bell hooks, *Talking Back: Thinking Feminist, Thinking Black* (Ontario: Between the Lines, 1989).

Staring Down the Tiger

Staring Down the Tiger

The tiger is a mythical creature in many cultures. It is revered for its strength and solitude. It has the ability to silently sneak up on an unsuspecting victim and consume it, either literally or metaphorically. The tiger is to be feared. It often represents death, for it can take life. In folklore, "A Girl, a Warrior, and a Tiger" tells of a Hmong girl who unintentionally lured a tiger to the village with her singing. The tiger hid along the edge of town, watching the Hmong. It wanted to possess their skill. Slowly, it killed every Hmong person in order to consume their talents. A shaman fought the tiger, and although he lost the battle, he learned what the tiger wanted. He told every Hmong to no longer share their talents in public or risk the tiger taking away their skills. Hmong are to be humble and not boast about their talents. The tiger still roams freely to this day. In the face of fear and mystery, it is better for one to retreat rather than fight the tiger. Do not agitate or awaken the tiger, or one could get bitten. Do not be boastful or "thaj loj" (show off), lest one be bitten. Do not sing unnecessarily or talk pointlessly; one could get bitten. Do not try to fight the tiger or approach it; you will be bitten.

The tiger sparks intrigue and curiosity. Hmong children are taught to stay away from the tiger, which in turn creates curiosity and childlike rebellion. Only an ignorant child would try to approach the tiger and get bitten. The phrase Hmong often use is "tigerbite," which means you were foolish and unwise for allowing yourself to get bitten by the tiger. You were stupid enough to approach the tiger and get bitten. You are a tigerbite.

The tiger might be feared for its strength and prowess, but it can easily be trapped and tricked. Although it was considered a formidable opponent, the tiger is also vulnerable to wit. In the folktale "The Woman and the Tiger," brothers set a trap and capture the tiger. In the folktale "Nine in One: Grrr! Grrr!" the tiger is tricked to believe that it can have only one baby in nine years—implying that although the tiger is strong, one can outsmart it. The tiger's vulnerabilities make it not entirely unapproachable.

The women in this book have turned that metaphor on its head. They are reclaiming the metaphor of the tiger. While they may fear the tiger, they have chosen to face it. They recognize that the tiger too has vulnerabilities. With honor and reverence, the women in this book choose to stare down the tiger. Instead of backing down and hiding our talents or stories for fear the tiger may consume us, we are staring down the tiger. We all have vulnerabilities. Writers explore the fear of speaking up and the impulse to hide one's talents; Gaosong V. Heu speaks eloquently about reclaiming the term *tigerbite*. Despite fears of the tiger, the women in this book choose to speak up. They found their voice and are staring down the tiger.

The book is organized into the following themes: A Woman's Journey, Ua Siab Ntev (Be Patient), Grand (Mothers) We Love, Moving through Cultures, and Breaking Barriers. Each theme captures the lived experiences of Hmong women as they journeyed from Laos to America, life in America, and pushing beyond barriers as bicultural women.

The themes are centered on different aspects of women's physical and psychological journey in their immigrant story. This journey came with loss of home, loss of family, and loss of loved ones. Women lost husbands, children, and many immediate and extended family members. They lost the homes they always knew, as well as their sense of belonging and community. Hmong women struggled to create a sense of home and belonging in their new country. As Hmong women developed new homes and communities for themselves, they struggled with the loss of competency and mastery over their own lives. Suddenly, they could not speak the language; they could not understand the culture and social norms. They had to rely on their children and strangers to complete everyday tasks.

They clung to memories of the Mekong River, water as a source of life and calm, yet the Mekong River was the site of death and turmoil for many Hmong. Pictures of loved ones are the only remaining mementos. Grave sites of loved ones who served in the war stand as reminders of our history and of the community's loss. For those born after the Secret War or in the United States, who have no real memory of the events in Laos and beyond, these memories were passed on.[1] There is a sense of loss for them as well; even in the absence of a true loss, they feel and embody the losses handed down by their parents and grandparents. They wade through these memories in search of their identities. The influence of Hmong women is revealed in these stories shared here by their children. The mother is honored for her love and sacrifice; in memories and stories about immigration, mother is poignant. Children take on the sorrow, loss, and memories of the women who came before them in order to connect to their origins.

Women lost their old selves, yet they could never claim their new selves in the United States, for they could never become truly American in a white supremacist world where to be American is to be white. Mothers struggled to understand their new culture and the new ways of life their American-born children so easily enjoyed. The women's lack of knowledge in the new world rendered them incompetent after having been competent leaders of their children and households. The stories give the reader a sense of loss, yet humor, as mothers struggled to understand their new world; although they detested some ways of their new home country, they knew there was no going back to the old ways. They learned to embrace the new. There were no written rules for how to confront their new world. As both narrators and subjects, these Hmong women are heroines, and their stories tell of ways in which they made sense of domestic violence and early marriage and how

---

1. The Secret War (1961–75) was a clandestine military effort conducted during the Vietnam War by the US government in northern Laos in which the American CIA engaged in efforts to intervene in external support from North Vietnamese Communist factions to Pathet Lao. Thousands of Hmong were recruited as soldiers. This effort led to the loss of many Hmong soldiers and the persecution of many Hmong following the end of the war in 1975.

they imposed psychological boundaries as a result of cultural boundaries. Hmong women tell of their sisters and mothers who went on to get an education in the United States and returned to their communities as leaders. These stories were hidden from us for a long time. This book seeks to shed light on these stories.

Introduction

Hmong arrived in the United States soon after the fall of Saigon in 1975. Hmong in the United States are mostly from Southeast Asia and were recruited as soldiers to fight alongside the Americans during the Secret War of the Vietnam era. Following the end of the war, thousands of Hmong refugees immigrated to the United States. The 2010 US Census counted more than 260,000 Hmong, encompassing three generations. The Hmong story is complex, containing pre- and post-migration struggles, intergenerational conflict, gender/familial role changes, and cultural transitions, among many other challenges. In that narrative are many untold stories from Hmong women and their children. This book aims to shed light on those stories, with themes that include experiences specific to Hmong women such as marriage, cultural transition, memory, loss, and breaking through barriers.

As immigrants, Hmong Americans have faced a variety of changes as they transitioned to life in the United States since 1976, changes that directly impacted gender roles and women within Hmong society. Work outside the home, education, and various other opportunities have significantly influenced the lived experiences of Hmong women in America. As Hmong women became involved in endeavors outside the home, they acquired educational degrees, celebrated careers and income advancements, and gained autonomy and voice about the direction of their day-to-day lives. These changes challenged traditional gender roles that once relegated women to being only wives, mothers, and daughters. Traditionally, the roles of wives, mothers, and daughters within Hmong society asked that women be subservient and focus on duties within the home to fulfill caretaking and childrearing responsibilities. As Hmong women gained the freedom and power to exercise notions of gender equality in which women experienced a higher level of autonomy and independence, the community as a whole faced challenges in maintaining the traditional expectations of women's roles within the home and community. Not without struggle and conflict, the Hmong American community has made great strides in adjusting to the changes in women's roles.

Exposure to Western notions of feminism does not imply that Hmong women did not already have wisdom around women's autonomy and gender equality. Western education did not "liberate" or "open the eyes" of Hmong women; Western education served as a springboard from which Hmong women were able to launch into and deepen their own understanding of their lived experiences, stories, and concepts as women. America's values around freedom and liberty contributed to and supported Hmong women's movement into liberation. Hmong women are still developing an understanding of feminism that embraces Hmong cultural nuances that dictate gender roles and bicultural lived experiences. When interpretations deviate from the white experience, they struggle to be normalized and recognized by the general population; thus, Hmong women need to tell their own stories and capture these stories in a platform to be consumed by mainstream society.

We are behooved to document and share Hmong women's stories that center on the themes of cultural change and immigration, the loss associated with those transitions, and how women have pushed past barriers in their journey. Current literature about the Hmong immigrant experience often focuses on the soldier story while omitting the narratives of Hmong women. This book provides a platform to tell these stories—stories that are often left unheard.

This anthology continues the work of collecting and documenting stories of Hmong women's journeys during their transition to the United States. Extant work in this area includes *Calling in the Soul: Gender and Cycle of Life in a Hmong Village* by Patricia Symonds (2004), *Culture and Customs of the Hmong* by Gary Yia Lee and Nicholas Tapp (2010), *An Introduction to Hmong Culture* by Ya Po Cha (2010), "Commentary: Gender-based Violence among the (H)mong" by Jacques Lemoine (*Hmong Studies*

Journal, 2012), *Claiming Place: On the Agency of Hmong Women* by Chia Y. Vang, Faith Nibbs, and Ma Vang (2016), and *The Bride Price: A Hmong Wedding Story* by Mai Neng Moua (2017). We stand on the shoulders of those before us as we stride forward in our journey to create lasting cultural, institutional, and social change to improve the lives of Hmong women.

PART 1

A Woman's Journey

Creating a Narrative for Hmong Women

Pa Der Vang

To be a catalyst for lasting cultural, institutional and social
change to improve the lives of Hmong women.
—Hnub Tshiab

At the age of forty-four, I am considered an elder in my community. Elder status is not only related to age in the Hmong community; it also has to do with experience and one's role. I am a
mother of two, I have a PhD in social work, and I've spent twenty
years volunteering for my community. These three factors have
contributed to my status as an elder. The story of my elder status has a lot to do with my work with Hnub Tshiab: Hmong
Women Achieving Together, an organization founded by a group
of Hmong women leaders in 1998 in St. Paul, Minnesota. Hnub
Tshiab's mission is to be a catalyst for lasting cultural, institutional, and social change to improve the lives of Hmong women.

I was born on a Thai military base that became a temporary
refugee camp for Hmong refugees fleeing Laos in 1975 after the
end of the Vietnam War. We became refugees because my father,
along with thousands of Hmong in Laos, fought alongside the
American CIA in the Secret War. When the United States lost the
war and pulled out of Laos, Hmong knew that they would be per-
secuted: we were freedom fighters and traitors at the same time.
My parents arrived in Missoula, Montana, when I was one year
old. I was a curious and observant Hmong daughter, which got
me into a lot of trouble. At the age of eight, I had the opportunity
to read Hmong folktales in my after-school Hmong language

Originally written for St. Catherine University, Center for Mission Blog,
February 26, 2018.

class. I was critical of one of our folktales, "Yao the Orphan Boy," in which the king's daughter married Yao, a poor orphan boy, and was told that if she was unhappy in her marriage, she was to find a broom and dustpan and sweep the whole house in order to find happiness. In her efforts to clean the house, she found a pot of gold and silver; thus, she and Yao were happy. I knew early on that this folktale was meant to teach girls that being a good Hmong wife would lead to happiness. Being a good Hmong wife involved, in my youthful mind, cleaning and housework and subservience. My young mind felt that there was more to life than just cleaning the house and serving my husband.

At that time, my school principal's name was Dr. Scott, and I was confused about why he wasn't practicing medicine. He explained the concept of a PhD to me, which encouraged me to pursue one of my own someday. As I began to forge my own way in life, I encountered much resistance from my community. I left a marriage at age twenty-three even though I knew it meant I would be ostracized; I was being selfish for leaving my family and focusing on my schooling instead. I lived on my own while in college despite claims that Hmong women who live alone are up to no good. While in college, I wanted to publish about Hmong women and the effects of traditional culture practices on the socioeconomic and mental health of Hmong women in the United States. I found that maintaining traditional practices such as teenage marriage and domestic servitude often inhibited Hmong women's socioeconomic and mental health later on in life. I encountered lots of resistance, but I continued my work and later published articles on this topic. Now I serve as a role model to other Hmong women who want to do the same type of research: I carved a path for them to do further work in this area.

While I was in school and volunteering, I felt very alone on my journey. I grew up during an era in which Hmong women did not question the status quo since the consequences for doing so were isolation, ostracization, ridicule, and even violence. Therefore, there were only a handful of women who spoke out about violence and oppression. In August 2000, while I was a graduate student, I came upon Hnub Tshiab: Hmong Women Achieving Together. This was a small group of Hmong women around the same age as me engaged in grassroots efforts to end domestic violence against Hmong women by ending sexism. I finally found my kindred spirits!

We boldly worked on ending sexism through the winter of 2006. We talked to people, published newsletters, gave talks, and spread the word, only to face criticism and threats from our community. However, the community wasn't ready to talk so explicitly about violence against women at that time, so we realized that we had to do something different. We had to go around the system, not through it. Following a 2006 retreat with more than fifty Hmong women in Sandstone, Minnesota, we found that the issues around violence and oppression against Hmong women remained unchanged.

Hnub Tshiab held a board retreat in the spring of 2007 and crafted a new mission. Instead of trying to end violence by changing sexism, we would be a catalyst for change by creating Hmong women leaders. We changed our mission to: "to be a catalyst for lasting cultural, institutional, and social change to improve the lives of Hmong women." We created the Hmong Women Leadership Institute, and we incorporated as a 501(c)(3) nonprofit organization in the same year. We changed our narrative. Instead of pounding on the problem of sexism, we focused on finding a solution for women. Instead of fighting a futile battle against age-old sexism, we would create Hmong women leaders as a solution. Changing the narrative was a powerful step in our organization's work. Today, we have completed the ninth year of our Hmong Women Leadership Institute, and we have graduated more than 108 Hmong women leaders who have gone on to create lasting cultural, institutional, and social change to improve the lives of Hmong women.

The story of my elder status has little to do with me. Although it is about me and my life, it has to do more with the journey of Hmong women. My life as a divorced mother of two resulted in ostracization, shame, and stigma, but this experience led me to my PhD and my studies about the effects of traditional practices on the lives of Hmong women in America, and finally to the work of developing Hmong women leaders through Hnub Tshiab: Hmong Women Achieving Together.

Top row, left to right: Mai Vang, Gao Thor, Yer Lor, Ma Vang, Ilean Her;
bottom row, left to right: Leona Thao, Pa Der Vang, Chee Lor, Cindi Yang

At the age of eight, in reading the story of "Yao the Orphan Boy," I knew that sweeping my house was a metaphor for being a good housewife. The pot of gold was the happiness I could find if only I could be a good wife. I knew that I would have to be brave if my pot of gold lay elsewhere. I also knew that I wasn't alone in this desire. I would have to look to the women who were already doing this work and continue to lay down bricks along the way for the Hmong girls who came after me. It wasn't an easy road, but it came with so many rewards. I found my pot of gold in my passion for my work and the relationships I forged along the way. I don't wish to change the folktale of "Yao the Orphan Boy"; I wish to add more to the story. In doing so, I became an elder.

Pa Der Vang is an associate professor in the department of social work at St. Catherine University. She has been a volunteer with Hnub Tshiab since August 2000. She publishes works on the immigration experience of Hmong in America.

How to Make Squirrel Stew

Pa Xiong

1. You start by cleaning the squirrels, exactly the way your mother had taught you all those years before.

You remember you had waited for your father to return home from his hunting trips in the Sierras, your father, who had often felt ashamed for not being able to provide a good life for you and your six siblings. In Laos, he had been an instructor of agriculture. He had made a respectable living. Here in America, he had become the recipient of welfare dollars; his children had become his teachers. You look at the two squirrels in front of you, the ones your brothers dropped off earlier today from their hunting trip before they headed home, and before you get to gutting the things, you take a second to be grateful first—for the Hmong men in your life. One knows this delicacy can't be bought at the supermarket.

2. Now, take a mini propane torch and burn off the fur.

Make sure there is enough distance between the squirrels and the flames. After all, you want to be careful not to melt the darn things. While your sisters sat around the house, your mother had asked only you to help her with the day's kill. She knew you weren't afraid to get your hands dirty, and you hadn't minded, anyway. Somebody had to hold on to this family recipe, and it might as well be you. Besides, you recall that your mother had made it a point to give every sibling his or her share of household tasks. She had even made your two older brothers help with kitchen chores. *How many other Hmong mothers made their sons clear away the dinner table after every evening meal?* You gather she taught your brothers something far more than they realized then. So, like you've seen your mother do so many times, pick up

17

the knife now, and scrape off all the charred fur. While Americans throw the skin away, we know, when cooked right, it is actually the best part.

3. After rinsing the squirrels, clean and gut them.

It is going to smell. Bad. But it won't faze you. It won't be any worse than the smell of manure all those early mornings you accompanied your parents to the pig farm in order to bring home freshly slaughtered meat. You had watched as the butchers electrocuted the animal, hung it by its legs, and then stabbed its neck to drain the blood. You may stop to question if you can do this part without your mother. But then, you will remember the time you overheard your father boasting about your academic achievements to his friends—"If she had been a boy," he said, "I would have been so proud." You know you have no choice now but to pick up the knife. You grip it just a little tighter and make a clean, steady cut, a vertical line down the abdomens of the squirrels. With one hand, you reach in and pull all the insides out. You do this without fear, without flinching.

4. Now, chop the squirrels into small pieces. Put them into a pot of boiling water.

Getting it to taste right will depend on the herbs and spices you use. You won't be able to buy all of the items at American supermarkets, but every Hmong family has a small garden where you will probably find exactly what you need. Lemongrass, Thai chili peppers, kaffir leaves. Just visit your parents' house. Make sure, though, that you have forgiven them for all the times you felt they loved your brothers more. Your father made you understand early on that being poor meant parents could not possibly give all their children the same things. That had also meant that what little they had to give had to go to their two sons first. You take a moment to feel fortunate that this tradition ends with you— neither your son nor your daughter will have to know these life lessons. Now find a local Asian supermarket and buy the remaining ingredients. Galangal root, Thai eggplant, fish sauce. With all the ingredients in the pot, you let it simmer. But not like the resentment that still brews inside of you. That, you will have to let go.

5. Share this stew with your four sisters.

You realize that much of who you are today is owed specifically to the women in your life. Whatever you all felt that you were lacking when you were younger, in fact, only made all of you stronger. In a family where boys were favored, your mother still found a way to give you and your sisters a small taste of equality, even if it had been simply to have your brothers help in the kitchen. However miniscule, she planted the seed. You know your life is changed because of it. So go ahead: invite your sisters over. You know they will appreciate it. Pass the wine glasses and make a toast to sisterhood. Girls aren't supposed to drink, so drink some more. Then spend the rest of the night sharing those god-awful stories from your youth. The five of you will find that laughing about your childhood is much more fun than crying about it. There is nothing to cry about today, after all. You just made Hmong squirrel stew, the way your mother had taught you all those years before.

Pa Xiong is a middle school English teacher living in southern California who holds bachelor's and master's degrees in Asian American studies. She spends most of her time raising her two kids, but here and there, when she can find a moment, she likes to write as well.

Soldier B31

Song Yang

I looked for you among the wall of black-and-white photographs, the most prominent feature in the *Hmongstory 40* exhibit. Forty years after the war, these hidden photographs have surfaced to showcase the many faces that might have been forgotten. I certainly have had you hidden in the back of my memory . . . but never forgotten.

I found your picture among the rows of unnamed soldiers. I had never seen this picture of you before, but I recognize the uniform. You walked through my village in your uniform, and all the girls thought you were so handsome. I couldn't believe you talked to me. We were teenagers when we got married . . . still so young when we had two sons.

Your cousins told me what happened the night you were sent to repair a broken telephone line. The enemy ambushed you. Grenades sprayed the air and blew off one of your legs. You were still alive but couldn't run. When they found you, they found stab wounds to

your head and chest. In your last moments, did you think about us? It's okay if you didn't. I know there wasn't much time. You and I never had much time. They brought your body to me to put into the ground. I buried you in a deep part of my memory.

I am not the same girl you married so many years ago. Sun spots sprinkle the surface of my face. Wrinkles wind their way from forehead to chin. You wouldn't recognize me. I am an old woman now, old enough to be your grandmother at the time of this photo. Death has taken a snapshot of you in time. Death has kept you young in my eyes.

The grandchildren ask, "Grandma, how do you know that's him?"

"Of course I know," I said. Some things I can't forget, and some things I struggle to remember.

I'm sorry.

I don't remember everything exactly. I am seventy years old now. I don't remember the sound of your voice. I don't remember dates or times or years. They all seem to blend together, fragmented at times, out of sequence, like a hard-to-remember dream.

I'm sorry.

I remarried. For love, not necessarily; for survival, certainly. I put away my tears for you. I took your sons away to the United States and left all evidence of you. When the war ended, it wasn't safe to be a soldier's wife. I burned all pictures of you, especially in uniform. This black-and-white photo is the first time I've seen your face outside of my own memory.

You were in my life for a short time, but look at what you left behind. Here are your grandsons: Bryan, Kevin, Sam, Jesse, and Eli. American names you wouldn't recognize; grandsons you'll never meet. They stare into your photo searching for something familiar in themselves.

You were not just a number. You were a mischievous son with dreams of being a pilot. You loved parachuting and outpaced your fellow soldiers. Your sister could not be consoled. You were her favorite. You have a story like so many other soldiers whose courage went unspoken. Resigned to your fate, your eyes still show defiance in the face of war. Defiance against silence.

I speak your name, Yia Yang. I carry your courage in my children and grandchildren as proof of survival. In this life, which has not always been so black and white, I've lived one truth. We survive not for those we've lost, but for those who need us to keep living.

Song Yang has a bachelor's degree in English from the University of Michigan and a master's in creative writing from the University of Wisconsin–Milwaukee. She enjoys teaching with technology and created the website www.hmongsewing.com to teach and preserve the tradition of sewing Hmong clothes and paj ntaub through online classes. She lives in Georgia with her husband and two kids.

The River

BoNhia Lee

Tell me a story.

These are the four magic words that drive the work of journalists, an editor once said, and the reason I became a reporter—a storyteller.

Over the last thirteen years, I have covered apartment fires, murders, real estate and development, business, and government and have written several stories about the refugee experience as told by Vietnamese, Bosnians, and those from different African countries. But I have never recorded my mom's tale.

Her journey to the United States, like that of many refugees, was a tragic one but is an inspiration for others to follow.

Life in the village was sweet, like the exotic fruit that hung from trees and the excitement of a small girl who got piggyback rides from her grandmother to the mountainside farm where she once picked the biggest cucumber of her life.

But the Secret War left the Hmong in turmoil. In 1975, when the United States pulled out of the Vietnam War, Mom and her family—her mother and six siblings—headed for the Mekong River to escape the Communists who were looking to detain Hmong from leaving the country. Her mom had secretly booked a boat ride across the river when it seemed they could no longer wait for her dad, who had traveled ahead to the Thai refugee camp to make sure it was safe.

The family hid overnight in an abandoned building next to the river. Half of the building was blown off during the war. The smell of sulfur from the bomb still lingered in the air, Mom said. At dawn, the family boarded a small motorboat with three men, a woman, and the boat operator.

The yellow Mekong River was dirty with mud, and there was debris floating in the fast current. It was the start of the rainy season. Mom sat in the front. Her two younger sisters and a brother sat in the middle, followed by her older sister, a brother, and her mother, who had a baby boy strapped to her back. The boat floated away from Vientiane, and Mom turned to watch the Thai shoreline inch closer. Then, water flooded the boat, creeping up over her feet and legs. She could hear screams and her mom praying, asking the sky above to help them survive.

Mom struggled to stay afloat as the boat sank beneath her. She could see her two younger sisters hanging onto baggage floating on top of the water. She bobbed up and down in the water for what seemed like forever before another boat pulled her to safety. Her two younger sisters and a brother were also later rescued.

I was in shock, very confused and did not know what
to think. I just stared mostly into space for many days.
I remembered trying not to [to] cry because if I cried, my
siblings would be scared. I had to take care of them.

They were taken to Nong Kai, a refugee camp created by the Thai government to house those escaping the war, where they were reunited with relatives and later their father, who had returned to Laos a day earlier to get the family.

There were no funerals for my grandmother, aunt, and uncles who drowned in the river while trying to escape. One uncle's little body was found floating in the river. He was wrapped in a grass mat and buried on the bank. Grandma's decomposed body was found two weeks later downstream. Mom was too sick to attend Grandma's burial and was told that Grandma was buried in a wooden casket.

It was the saddest time of my life. Half of my family
was gone in an instant. I was living in a nightmare that
I wanted to wake up from but could not. Until this day,
I still dream about my mother being missing all this time
and someone in Thailand found her.

Life in the camp wasn't easy. Mom, who was about ten years old, would only buy food for her five-year-old brother. Her two younger sisters ate the leftovers, and Mom ate whatever was left. Her brother got very sick from the river water he swallowed and had diarrhea for weeks. Mom would wake up several times at night to take her brother to the outhouse in the dark. When he couldn't make it, Mom would dig a hole to bury his stool.

Mom and her family lived in the camp from May 1975 to October 1976; then they boarded a bus to Bangkok and a plane to the United States. She remembers landing in Fort Wayne, Indiana, and seeing yellow and orange leaves. She was sure she would not like the United States.

But Mom picked up English fast and began interpreting for relatives at medical appointments and hospital visits. She married at age sixteen and a year later had me—the first of three children. She would eventually earn her nursing degree while working and caring for the family. She's been a nurse for almost thirty years now.

Yet being a floor, emergency room, and urgent care nurse wasn't enough; she wanted to do more. Mom returned to Thailand a few years ago with a Hmong medical mission team (and has since participated on medical missions to Haiti, Panama, the Philippines, and Kenya) to help the sick and to heal her own heart.

> We stopped [by the Mekong River] to pay respect and say goodbye to my family members who I lost many years ago that I never had the chance to say goodbye to.

She threw flowers into the murky water.

I will never experience such tragedy. But I can record it and share it with others.

BoNhia Lee is a communications specialist at Fresno State writing about student and faculty success, research, and other university accomplishments. She was previously a journalist for fifteen years. BoNhia contributed to the Fresno Bee's "Living in Misery" special report on substandard housing that launched citywide debate in Fresno, California, and earned a George F. Gruner Award for public service. Born and raised in Syracuse, New York, BoNhia graduated from the S. I. Newhouse School of Public Communications at Syracuse University. She is married with three children. BoNhia credits her mother's leadership and story for inspiring her to become a journalist.

The White Roses

Duabhav BJ Lee

Maybe I wanted something peaceful and beautiful to acknowledge the changing of a generation. The death of the Hmong leader General Vang Pao in January 2011 left me in a panic as I thought of the elders in my mother's generation. Those who lost their lives fighting for this unknown world of democracy and those still fighting for the American Dream with twelve-hour shifts.

I laid a half dozen long-stemmed white roses at the meager Secret War Memorial at Arlington Cemetery the day I learned about General Vang Pao's death. I wondered if the baby's breath that adorned those white roses was fresh. I wanted to make sure that I honored his death properly. With my phone, I took a photo of those flowers and texted it to my mom.

Five years later, I sat listening to my uncle Laotoua describe how he orchestrated our family's escape from Laos. I wondered what my mother thought of her escape with Uncle and his family. I thought of the white roses.

The photo of the white roses that I texted to my mother eventually made its way back to me. I found the picture on my mom's phone. She kept it on her phone all these years even though she had gone through five phones. My mother loves her photographs. I paused as I reflected on hearing the story of my family's escape from Laos, then finding the picture of the flowers on my mom's phone. Maybe this is God's way of bringing everything together.

I remember the corner market I often rushed past each day on my way to work. How my boss let me go home early that day, and how by chance I walked into the store, not sure what I was looking for. The white roses, my mother's favorite, caught my eye, and I knew they needed to go with me. The metro from U Street to Arlington was sparsely populated. The ride seemed too short as I clutched the flowers in my arms and thought of my parents.

It made the most sense to me to go to Arlington Cemetery that day, a place oddly out of place but tucked into the hearts of every American who has ever served our country. It was chilly as I stepped off the platform. I found my way to the entrance, and with a bit of courage I walked slowly toward the memorial. It had been only a few months since my parents and I had come to pay our respects to the soldiers of the Secret War, when I started my position in Washington, DC. I stood, slowly breathing in the cool air that took my breath away. I wasn't sure if I should say anything. I don't recall if I managed to mutter any words of condolence to the engraved golden lettering before me. Alone and yet together with my Hmong family and loyal allies near and far, I placed the roses and brushed the memorial with my freezing fingers. Every time we visited Grandma's grave, Mother always pulled off the twigs and weeds. This was the closest I could get to my Hmong tears weeping across the country and the world.

My mother loves white roses. She kept the picture of the white roses not only because she loves photographs but because our mothers are the keepers of our histories. I chose the white roses in honor of my mother, in honor of the soldiers of the Secret War.

Duabhav BJ Lee is a born and raised Hmong southern belle trying to write about what moves her, shakes her, and makes her laugh.

Lub Ntuj Tshiab: Under a New Sky

Kia M. Lor

At first this was a letter to my mother. Now it is a story about us.

I'm standing on a peak on the highest mountain range in the world, the Himalayas, and all I can see is you, *Niam* (Mom). Of course you aren't here with me on this fine April day. You are on the opposite side of the world, back home in America. It is the first time in my twenty years of life to be this far from home, to be under this new sky. *Niam*, you aren't physically here with me, but you are mentally here in every detail I see. I can see your face in the majestic mountains. I can taste the health you brag about in the fresh and clear streams. Now I understand why you always complimented the American roads; here the rigid roads are filled with rocks, pebbles, and potholes. I can hear your voice at the back of my mind, saying, "Minnesota is so flat, my child; you are missing out on the beautiful nature I grew up in." Women are carrying heavy firewood on their backs, kids are running around naked, and families have hung their wet clothes outside on the clothesline to dry. I don't fit in this place. My back is not strong enough to bear this heavy firewood. My clothes are too thick to dry on the line. I don't belong under this sky. This sky is foreign to me, but I know it's familiar to you.

Niam, you used to tell me the story of how we left the refugee camp in Phanat Nikom, Thailand, how we boarded an airplane, had two layovers—one in Tokyo and the other in Los Angeles—and landed in Minnesota with our one-way tickets. It was in the summer of 1995, and I was four years old. You were twenty-six years old and nine months pregnant with Gao Chia. You gave birth to her shortly after we landed in St. Paul, making Gao Chia the first person in our family to become a US citizen. You named her Gao Chia (*Nkauj Tshiab*, literally translates to "New Girl") because we were in a new world.

St. Paul became our new permanent home. As much as you detested the Whoppers at Burger King, there was no turning back
for you. The ten thousand lakes did not fascinate you. The Mall
of America bored you. There were no mountains or crystal-clear
rivers in St. Paul. July turned to December, and the snow buried
the earth with icy, cold, white fluff. That was when you came to
know that we couldn't wear flip-flops outside; instead, we needed
winter boots and coats (which we couldn't afford). You said icy,
cold, white fluff on earth was abnormal. I believed you. *Naturally.*

But in third-grade science class I learned that the Earth is
tilted at a 23.5-degree angle, which is why we have four seasons:
spring, summer, autumn, and winter. The pattern of the seasons
in Minnesota was normal, much like the snow falling from the
sky in December. That was when *you* became "abnormal," *Niam.*
You became abnormal because you believed people should drive
on the left side of the road. You became abnormal for thinking
that flushing the toilet was scary. You became abnormal because
you questioned why every house had a TV, why people mowed
their lawns, why people showered in a bathtub with shower
curtains, why we had to pay rent every month and document
everything on paper. Because you kept reminding me about how
odd these things were, you eventually became the outcast. You
didn't fit in this place; you didn't belong under the American sky.

Because you were always out of place, you frustrated me while
I was growing up. I kept comparing you to other mothers, questioning why you couldn't be more normal like them. Why were
you so dependent on everyone? You married three times to three
abusive men who didn't have large enough hearts to love your
children, just so you could depend on their help. Why couldn't
you drive? You forced me to take driver's education so I could get
my license at sixteen in order to drive the family around. Why
couldn't you speak English? I still remember visiting your psychologist when I was only in third grade. Your translator was
late to the appointment, so I had to translate the first part. Since
I was able to comprehend a little English, you thought I knew
enough to inform the psychologist that you were stressed out.
In Hmong, *stress* is *nyuab siab*, literally translated as "difficult or
heavy liver." I shyly and reluctantly told the psychologist with
my childlike English, "My mom say she have very heavy heart,"

knowing that the sentence would only make sense if I used *heart* instead of *liver*. At the time, I was upset at myself for not knowing the English definition for *stress*; later, I became upset at you for setting me up to fail, though you didn't know that I'd failed.

You couldn't support me educationally, and the distance between us grew wider. I worked hard to achieve academic success in school. Third grade left, and twelfth grade came in 2009. It was senior year, and I was at the apex of my academic game. I surged into the top ten percent of my class and earned myself a six-year, full-ride Gates Millennium Scholarship to any college in the United States. I remember that spring night in May: we sat in front of Mrs. Lynch for a parent-teacher conference at Johnson High School; I found myself translating—again.

At one point during the conference, Mrs. Lynch said, "Kia is a phenomenal student. She is very studious and polite. Many people adore her. She never misbehaves, and she completes all her assignments on time. Kia is a great person, and it was wonderful having her in class." She ended by saying, "You should be proud that Kia is your daughter."

I nodded and smiled at Mrs. Lynch's compliments. Then I turned toward you, *Niam,* and looked at your numb, blank, stolid face; you were unable to recognize the huge vocabulary Mrs. Lynch used. My lips went numb. Suddenly my face burned red. I became shy. Ashamed. How in the world was I supposed to translate to you all these great things about me? How was I supposed to brag about myself like this in front of you? I couldn't find the courage to tell you these things; plus, culturally, you've taught me to not be so vain. Three seconds passed by as I lowered my head and looked at my shoes and condensed all of Mrs. Lynch's words into six simple Hmong words: *"Nws hais tias kuv keej heev"* (She said that I'm very talented). Again, I blamed you for not understanding English in the first place. If you knew English, then I would not have to fight with myself like this.

I became more frustrated when you couldn't understand why I wanted to go to college an hour and a half away from home. You wanted me to stay home, to stay close to you. Hmong sons could venture into the world, but Hmong daughters were forbidden to leave the home. You know me, *Niam,* and you know how much I detested these Hmong gender restrictions. I defied you and went away. I thought distancing me from you was the solution. But *Niam*, the farther I go away from you, the closer you become. You have no idea how much this distance has changed how I see you.

All my life, I've only seen you as the Hmong woman under the sunlight of *my* sky in America. I've only seen an unstable woman who could not fend for herself. With a blindfold over your eyes and hopes under your breath, you left the refugee camps of Thailand and came to the United States, a country where the "American Dream" is far from your reach. Yet, *Niam*, it never occurred to me that you were a professional fire-starter, banana-tree-chopper, firewood-carrier, rice-field-cutter, and hand-laundry-washer. You left your bamboo hut to come to a four-walled concrete building. Naturally you would be unstable in America; naturally you would lose that talented strong woman you were to the alien world of America.

Today, on this high mountain range, your voice plays like music at the back of my mind: *"Kuv coj nej tuaj rau teb chaws Mekas kom nej pom kev vam meej es nej thiaj tsis txom nyem li kuv"* (I brought all of you to America so you can see opportunities and possibilities and will not have to suffer from poverty like me). The greatest thing you've given me and my brothers and sisters is an escape route away from war in the refugee camps in Thailand. You gave us the world. I wish you were standing on this Himalayan mountain next to me. It's such a beautiful view, *Niam*.

I stand here imagining how I might share this epiphany with you when I return home. I picture you and me alone in the kitchen because that is the only place where we can have civil conversations. In the kitchen you were my teacher and I was your student. You would be boiling chicken for dinner, your spoon hitting the side of the pot as you stir salt and black pepper into the broth. I would be rinsing the jasmine rice twice, then putting it in the rice cooker and pressing it down to cook. Our backs would be turned toward each other. We have never been able to meet eye to eye, but we would be able to listen ear to ear. In the silence I would work up the courage to tell you that I was standing on the highest mountain range in the world, and it was the most beautiful view ever, and on that mountain peak it hit me that you've climbed a much higher mountain than that one. In fact, you've climbed many mountains higher than Everest; you've seen more of the world than I give you credit for. And I would apologize for blaming you for everything. I'd take back the excruciating words I'd thrown at you, each like a dagger into your heart. One by one I would take out those daggers and heal your wounds. All these years I blamed you for my flaws and the things I couldn't do. I blamed you that I couldn't shop at the mall because we were too poor, so instead we shopped at the thrift store. I blamed you for not having grand birthday parties for me, not having a home I could bring my friends to, not being able to communicate with my teachers at conferences. I blamed you for making me responsible for paying the bills. I blamed you for being weak and dependent on men—I never dated because seeing your relationships terrified me. But I take it all back. You never asked for any of this, Niam. I would turn around and see you standing there smiling at me with your short gray hair and the forty-four-year-old wrinkles around your dark brown eyes. You would say to me that I was everything you wanted me to be and that you knew all along I was going to realize it on my own. We would be liberated from our haunting past.

But in reality I know I'll return home and be busy unpacking my four month's-worth of belongings from India and repacking to head out to college again. I'll use my "busyness" as an excuse to mask my emotions because I will be too shy to tell you that I saw your face in the mountains. It'd be too strange for you to hear it, too; you wouldn't know how to cope with my epiphany.

At first this was a letter to you, Niam, my mother. Now it is a story about us.

A story you will probably never read.

Kia M. Lor was born in a Thai refugee camp and came to the United States with her family when she was four years old. She is the second of six children and the eldest daughter. At a young age, Kia acquired skills to be a cultural broker between her immigrant mother and the mainstream American culture. Today, she acts as an academic cultural broker as assistant director of Language and Intercultural Learning at the Fries Center for Global Studies at Wesleyan University in Middletown, Connecticut. Kia is also an active fellow at the Intercultural Communication Institute in Portland, Oregon.

Lub Neej Paj Ntaub

Tou SaiKo Lee

In honor of the Hmong women in our lives

VERSE 1

Thaum tsis muaj kev cia siab, kuv niam nyob ntawv,
When there was no hope, my mother was there,

Hais cov lus pab kuv, tu kuv tus kheej, yog lawm,
Saying words to help me take care of myself, that's right.

Xav txog ua niam hauv lub neej no tsis yooj yim,
I think about how being a mother in this life is not easy,

Tsis muaj ib zaug, tsis nco, ua tsaug rau ib sim,
There is never a time I would forget, thank you forever.

Niam siv zog ua hauj lwm, tseem saib xyuas me nyuam,
Mom strives to work hard, still takes care of children;

Muam, rau siab kawm ntawv tseem pab tu tsev luam,
Sister studies for school, still helps take care of the home;

Pog ua zaub mov noj, qhia dab neeg kom luag ntxhi,
Grandma makes meals, tells stories for us to smile.

Me nyuam ntxhais nyeem ntawv, khiav ua si kom luag ntxhi,
Daughter reads books, runs to play to make us smile.

Zoo li tsis muab vaj huam sib luag, mloog, mi ntsis,
Seems like there is no equality, listen a little bit:

34

Thaum yug los loj hlob, muaj co saib poj niam qis
Growing up from childhood, there are some who see women
    as lower,

Muaj neeg hais tias, txiv neej yog cov muaj nuj nqis,
Someone said, "men are the ones with value,"

Tab sis tsis muaj niam thiab pog, tsis muaj txoj kev kho
But if there wasn't Mom and Grandma, there would be no
    way to heal.

Tsis muaj peb cov ntxhais, ces leej twg yuav hlub koj?
If there wasn't our daughters, who would love you?

Xav txog tus phauj txais tau nyiaj mus kawm ntawv deb,
Think about the auntie who received money to go to college
    far away,

Lawv hais kom nws yuav txiv, yug me nyuam, nyob tsev,
They told her to get married, have children, and stay home;

Xav txog tus muam lawv yuam yuav txiv thaum yau,
Think about the sister they forced to get married too young,

Yug me nyuam, tus txiv qaug cawv, muab nws ntaus,
Had children, the husband got drunk and assaulted her;

Xav txog niam tu siab, tus txiv tham ib tug tshiab,
Think about the mother's misery, her husband trying to find
    a new love,

Hlub tus nyob nplog teb, ua tsev neeg puas tas,
He loves another one in Laos, his family is broken,

Tseem xa nyiaj thiab, me nyuam nyuaj siab tas,
He even sends money, children are all depressed;

Lub neej poob zoo, pab tsis tau lawv tus keej,
Their lives are lost, unable to help themselves.

Ua cas xuaj ua luaj, li ntawv tsis muaj neeg yeej,
Why so shameful, hence no one will win,

Vim li cas lawv ntxub poj niam, tsis muaj kev hlub?
Why do they hate women, there is no love?

Yuav tsum nhriav txoj kev tshiab, hwm txoj kev qub,
Need to find a new way, honor the old ways,

Yog peb xav mus deb, pab txhawb nqa lawv tom ntej,
If we want to go far, help support them in the future,

Tsis muaj lawv yug peb, tsis muaj kev hauv ntiaj teb.
If they didn't give birth to us, there would be no existence in
    this world.

CHORUS

Paj Ntaub, tsis muaj kev ncaj ncees rau peb hais,
Our story cloth, there is no justice for us to speak,

Xav txog koj pog, koj niam, cov muam, cov ntxhais.
Think about your grandma, your mom, the sisters, and the
    daughters.

Qhib siab, koom tes, thov kom peb, xav tom ntej.
Have an open mind, get together, let's all think progress,

Me nyuam yuav ua raws li peb, lawv yuav ua raws li peb.
Children will do what we do; they will be influenced by us.

VERSE 2

Muaj ib co tsis siab zoo, kuv twb ntsib ob peb tug,
There are some who are not good hearted; I have met a few.

Thov nej xav txog cov poj niam muaj kev hlub.
I ask you to think about the women who have love (for you).

Txiv neej zoo, xav kom nej ua suab nrov,
Good men, need you to have a louder voice,

Sawv los, txog caij qhia sawv daws paub txog.
Stand up: it's time to teach everybody to know about this.

Pab cov muam ua suab luag, hais txiv neej hnov,
Help the sisters have laughter, speak to (other) men to hear,

Ib co muaj teeb meem, muaj kev sib ceg,
Some have problems and there are arguments,

Tsis sib haum, nrhiav kom tau, txoj kev zoo, yav tom ntej.
Don't get along, try to find a way to be better in the future.

Ua siab loj, xav txog me nyuam lub neej ua ntej,
Be understanding, think about the children's lives first,

Thaum txiv ntaus tus niam, tsis muaj kev haum xeeb.
When a father hits a mother, there is no peace.

Mloog cov lus, nkag siab niam txoj kev txom nyem,
Listen to the words, understand mothers' struggles,

Saib hom phiaj uake, hloov kev xav hauv ntiaj teb.
Plan goals together, change the way we think in this world.

Ib co ua thawj coj, kom lawv muaj npe nrov,
Some people become leaders so they can be famous,

Ib co siv zog, pab cov neeg hauv teb chaws no,
Some people make an effort to help others in this country,

Xav pom cov mus deb, tig rov qab los nco,
Want to see those who succeed give back and remember,

Txhawb cov phauj, ua thawj coj, kub siab,
Support Auntie who is a devoted leader,

Tu cov tub loj hlob, kom saib taus poj niam,
Raise the boys to grow up and respect women,

Sib kho, tag nrho, kom peb tau kev vam meej.
Heal each other, all of us, so we can have prosperity.

Yuav tsum hwm cov poj niam hauv peb lub neej.
Need to honor the women in our lives.

Tou SaiKo Lee is a spoken word poet, storyteller, hip-hop recording artist, and community organizer from St. Paul, Minnesota. He has facilitated songwriting/performance poetry workshops and residencies at schools and community centers in ten US states and in Thailand. Tou SaiKo received the Jerome Foundation Travel and Study Grant in 2008, an Intermedia Arts VERVE Spoken Word grant in 2009, and a Bush Foundation Fellowship in 2016 to utilize arts to preserve cultural identity. He is writing a memoir about his collaboration with his grandmother and is working on his first Hmong-language hip-hop album, Ntiaj Teb Koom Tes, *which translates to* Unified Worldwide.

PART 2

Ua Siab Ntev

On Choice

Lyncy Yang

"Kuv yog ib tug menyuam yaus xwb thaum kuv niam lawv muab kuv muag, mus yuav txiv." *I was just a child when my mother sold me off to a husband.* The way my mother tells it, she was barely into her double digits before being sold off for money and goods.

"Lawv ntshaw nyiaj." *They coveted money.*

Naive me used to ask her why she didn't just say no, stubbornly plant herself in the middle of the floor in front of all the relatives and refuse to leave the house. Her parents were bound to give in if she were determined enough, right?

She always repeated that she couldn't be like us and refuse.

"Well, run away!"

She'd laugh and ask, "Where would I run to?" Refusing was not an option; the only option was to conform to everyone else's expectations, wants, and needs. My heart sinks at how terrified she must have been to follow orders, transfer authority to a stranger, and spend the first night in an unfamiliar bed, with an unknown man, listening to his orders as darkness fell.

My mother was a victim of circumstance, but a persistent one. In time, her husband became familiar, her lifeline, her first love. (While he was the love of her life, he was not, however, her only lover.)

She held on to him tightly—bowed to his will and ways. That is, until death gripped him harder than she could and made him—and her—bend to its will and ways. Sending her dead husband into the spirit world was the first most tragic thing that happened in her life—more tragic than being forced to marry a complete stranger.

I think losing her husband to death—something she could not control—fostered an unflinching disposition toward the men who willingly chose to leave my mother at their own whim.

Death, she couldn't compete with. Choice, she could. So, she was never going to try to keep a man around when she knew what true loss was. They weren't dying, disappearing into the vast unknown world of spirits and ancestors; they were choosing to walk away from her, and she was not going to run after them and grip on to something that had no intention of staying in the first place. Their choices could never carry the weight of her first husband's death, so they were no real loss to her. She gained more than she lost: two children. One each from two separate relationships.

My mom carried the lesson of an early forced marriage in her guidance, love, and care for me. The first time I truly felt this in all of its complicated ways was when I was sixteen.

I changed into a pair of navy sweatpants and an oversized T-shirt in my basement bedroom after getting home from being out with my mentor, Lu. My mom enthusiastically trotted through the shadow of the basement hallway as she spoke into the phone. Her bright smile and spirited tone revealed that good news had just greeted her.

Mom's joyful spirit always boosted my mood. Eager to hear who was on the opposite end of the receiver, I asked through my smile, "Ab tsi na?" *What is it?*

"Nrog koj tus nus Zong tham os." *Speak with your brother Zong.*

"Zong yog leej twg na?" *Zong is who?*

"Ah! Yog koj ib tug cous-ing na." *He's one of your cousins.*

I'd better not ask too many questions and piss her off. I'll just figure it out on my own and ask him myself.

I grabbed the phone from her ear. "Hello?" I introduced myself. Told him I was sixteen.

In Hmong, he asked if I was looking forward to meeting him. "Me leej muam, vam thiab cia siab wb tau sib ntsib os, yom?"

In English, I replied, "Of course I am excited; you're a relative. Can't have too many of those." I asked him who he was exactly, how we were related.

He explained that he was a close cousin on my mom's side.

"Oh! Puas yog mas?!" *Oh, really?!* I pretended to know who he named off. "Es thaum twg koj mas tuaj saib peb os?" *When will you come visit us?*

"In less than a week. I'm looking forward to meeting you," he responded in English.

"Me too, cousin!" Something told me I had to establish some boundary between us, letting him know that all he could ever be to me was a relative. Never a lover.

"Koj puas muaj hluas nraug?" *Do you have a boyfriend?*

"Uh, no." I quickly changed the subject and asked if he was traveling with anyone—his kids, wife? "Koj puas coj koj poj niam thiab me nyuam tuaj saib peb os?"

"Ib tug kwv tij," he said. *Another relative.*

The conversation did not last long after that. I don't remember exactly how it unfolded, but I remember leaving the call unsure of whether the tone of his voice was brotherly, cousinly love or a nasty attempt to seduce me into romance. The exaggerated softness of his voice (what our elders would call "qab zib" or *sweet*) felt artificial, fraudulently kind. It made my gut churn.

I shook away the thought of him casting any romantic interest my way and gave him the benefit of the doubt. *He's my cousin; that would be gross.*

A week later, he appeared in black trousers and a white-and-blue-striped polo with another short Hmong man in his sixties sporting a black suit and white button-up shirt. Mom introduced me to him and told me he was the cousin I talked to on the phone. They both would be staying with us for the week, in my room. I'd sleep with my mom in her bed for the meantime.

Not a problem; I obliged.

The story slowly unfolded. He was in Minnesota to look for a wife, and his companion was his *mej koob* (middleman or officiator in planning a wedding). If and when Zong found his match, his *mej koob* would start the Hmong nuptials between her family and Zong. Marry them quickly.

Their trip, to me, felt like a business trip. They were here to acquire an asset—another human body—for him to invest in, take home, and create a profitable life of babies, money, and companionship. I wondered if maybe the love would accrue and compound like interest.

Each day during dinner, my mom would eagerly ask if he found a potential match. Each of his interactions, as he described the women he met, was like betting on a random hand of baccarat. He never seemed quite sure if he was going to win or lose, if the women were going to wager or fold.

I often wondered how love could be left to such chance in so many traditional Hmong marriages. I ruminated on my mother during these dinner conversations and wondered if she really had an interest in any of her husbands after her first marriage—especially if they were forced on her like a losing hand in baccarat.

Zong was on a time crunch. He had to return to work. His days were limited, and he was losing time and money. The investment of his and his *mej koob*'s labor proved to be unfruitful.

On the last evening before his departure, I came home to find Zong and his *mej koob* sitting knee to knee, heads leaning in toward each other in a concentrated, muffled exchange of words. They resembled two young children plotting how to go about a secret mission—neither completely on the same page with the other.

I joined my mother in the kitchen and greeted her. "Hi, Mommy."

"Hi. Pab kuv rau mov noj." *Help me set the table.*

"Okay." I opened the rickety oak veneer drawers to pick out spoons and forks.

Zong's *mej koob* entered from the opposite end of our galley kitchen to speak with my mother. Stepping over the threshold of the adjoining dining room, I heard the *mej koob* speak over the whirring noise of the stove fan, "Niam tij, Zong yuav yuav koj tus ntxhais xwb laiv." *Older sister-in-law, Zong insists on only marrying your daughter.*

Oh, that isn't me, I told myself as I looked down on the spoons and forks I was setting at each place on the dinner table.

Silence. My eyes elevated to meet my mother's face full of pause. She rarely ever looked at a loss for words, but her twisted brow and cocked head revealed stun and puzzlement from the *mej koob*'s words.

"Tus ntxhais twg?" *Which daughter?*

"Koj tus ntxhais yau." *Your youngest daughter.*

Shit, that's me. Right? I was suddenly unsure whether I was her youngest daughter. Was there a younger daughter I didn't know about, or a cousin somewhere? I'm sure in that exact moment of realization, I was wide-eyed, mid-breath.

"Av." *Oh.* She glanced at me, never fully making eye contact, and let out a laugh of relieved disbelief. It was as if she had complete control of this moment and knew exactly how to handle it.

She replied cheerfully, and ever so kindly, "He doesn't want to marry her. She's too young and doesn't know anything. She can't even prepare a meal. She's still a child and is not ready to be a wife. I will not allow her to marry right now. We're one family, so don't think ill of my decision."

Zong sat silently in the living room as he listened from the safety of our couch. The *mej koob* did not argue or seek to negotiate. Perhaps he understood the ridiculousness of such a proposition. He shuffled back into the living room to relay the message to Zong in whispers. There was more muffled talk between the two of them.

I wavered back into the kitchen for plates and searched for an indication in my mother's face that she meant what she said: she wouldn't let me marry . . . him, or anyone else for that matter. That she looked out for me, protected me and my interests. That she believed in what she had just said and wouldn't go back on her word.

She smiled at me, squeezed her eyes and shoulders in, and mouthed, "Shh"—code for *we'll talk about it later.*

We gathered for a final dinner together with my brothers and sisters and tried our very best to make it as loving and natural as possible before our guests' departure.

At the end of our night, she asked me as I was getting into bed, "Koj puas ntshai?" *Were you scared?*

"Yeah," I admitted. I told her I thought it was gross he wanted to marry me. "He's so old and has kids," I chortled.

She said that, traditionally, it would have been good to have him marry me; then she'd know he would love me, the family, and her. I still contended that such an arrangement was ludicrous and disgusting. She gently smiled, as if withholding a secret to life—perhaps she was smiling at my naivete, or at being able to protect me from what her mother and father wouldn't when she was a child.

She never fully explained why she didn't approve of that marriage proposal. In my most basic understanding, it was because I was young, he was too old, and I was not in love. But I think she knew what it was like to be sold off without a chance to really live and be loved. To know the abandonment of your most trusted and be the cursed casualty of circumstance. As a mother fully in control, she was going to do right by her kids. Her grip tightened around each of us—especially her daughters—because of her conviction and her belief held for our individual freedom. Having lost her first love to the inescapable enemy called death, she wasn't going to lose us to choice.

Lyncy Yang was born and raised in St. Paul, Minnesota. A product of her family, city, and community, she aspires to chronicle the stories of family, food, and the complexities as well as the simplicities of living as a Hmong woman and community member. She is a sister, a daughter, and a proud aunt to many nieces and nephews, who all inspire her to be a better human being every day. An educator, writer, cook, gardener, and traveler, she hopes to combine her many identities, passions, and aspirations to make meaningful contributions to her local and global community.

Because I Love You

Pa Der Vang

"You don't love me."
> *"I do love you."*

"If only you were a boy."

"You need to learn how to cook. No one will marry you if you don't know how to cook."
> *"If he won't marry me because I can't cook, then that's his loss."*

"You need to learn how to be still and cross your legs when you sit down, like your cousins."
> *"Why do girls have to cross their legs?"*

"Why can't your brothers help me pull up the tree roots from my garden?"
> *"I've been helping you all day. I almost chopped my shin with that ax."*

"If only you were a boy."

"I can only count on my sons to love me when I get old."
> *"The daughters can take care of you, too, just like the boys."*

"You are too skinny. You need to eat more."
> *"When I was in Laos, they knew I was American because of my plumpness."*

"You got fat. Don't eat so much."
> *"You said fat is good."*

"Don't eat so much. They will call you hu dab (big appetites will summon the spirits) when you get married."
> *"What if I'm hungry?"*

"You need to learn how to sew paj ntaub so you can sew Hmong clothes for yourself when you get older."
> *"Maybe I can borrow yours or I can just buy it."*

"Why is your paj ntaub all brown! You didn't wash your hands!"

47

"I don't know how you keep it so white, Mom."

"You need to wear Hmong clothes to Hmong New Year."

"It's too tight and heavy. I can't breathe, and the necklace leaves a bump on my neck."

"You have to ball toss at Hmong New Year. I did it when I was your age."

"But they are all old men. That is disgusting."

"Who is that man who gave you flowers at Hmong New Year? You're going to get knuckled (mag khauj tsiav!)."

"You wanted me to ball toss so why are you shocked that someone gave me flowers?"

"You have to go dance with Uncle. He wants to dance with you."

"But I'm fourteen, and he looks like he's thirty."

"You should marry my nephew."

"That's gross."

"If you marry my nephew, they will love you because you are family."

"You have to serve him a drink. He is our guest."

"Why do girls have to serve?"

"Why are you talking to him? Do you want to marry him or something?"

"No. Women can talk to men without wanting to marry them."

"Don't marry a white man. You're to marry a Hmong man. A white man won't love you."

"I'll marry someone I love."

"Why do you have to be so hard-mouthed (tawv ncauj)?"

"I'm not tawv ncauj. I'm just stating my opinion."

"If you don't listen, I will twist your ear (mag ntswj pob ntseg)."

"If you twist my ear, I'll tell my teacher and child protection will come take me."

"If you want to go live with white people, then go ahead."

"Why do you ask so many questions? You're supposed to know already."

"But how am I supposed to know if you don't teach me?"

"Why did you cancel your landline? Are you moving in with someone? You're bringing shame onto us."

"No one uses a landline anymore."

"You need to get married soon. You're getting old."

"But I'm only fourteen!"

"Why did you get married? You were supposed to finish school first."

"You've been asking me to marry since I was fourteen."

"Why do you have the lights on so late at night? You're wasting electricity!"

"I have to get my reading done, and I still have so much homework."

"Turn off the lights now or you will get in big trouble!"

"Why is it taking you so long to finish college? Are you really going to school?"

"It takes several years to get a college degree."

"I'm glad we let you go to school."

"You didn't LET me go to school."

"The world will say we didn't help you through school."

"They will say I did it for you."

"If only you were a boy, you would be a leader."

"I don't yearn to be a leader."

"Your divorce shamed us."

"Divorce is awful, but it is pretty common."

"It's a good thing you divorced him because you wouldn't have finished school if you stayed."

"That's true."

"Mom I'm dating someone, and he's white."

"You're so old now. As long as he is a good man, that's okay. You need to get married or no one will bury you."

"I am considering cremation."

"You will come back all burnt."

"Mom, why did you make it so hard for me when I was growing up?"

"Because I love you."

Pa Der Vang is an associate professor in the department of social work at St. Catherine University. She has been a volunteer with Hnub Tshiab since August 2000. She publishes works on the immigration experience of Hmong in America.

Kuv Niam

Gao Vang

My mother was born in the northern hills of Laos. As a child, after a day of playing in the fields, careful not to stray far for fear of encountering tigers or soldiers, my mother ran home to devour a pile of *ncuav pob kws* that my great-grandmother stacked in the middle of the floor for her. Corn pancakes were my mother's favorite growing up. My great-grandparents looked after my mother and auntie during the day, while my grandmother farmed and sold vegetables at the market in the village.

My mother has one older sister. They are half sisters, but love each other in full since they were born from the same womb and drank from the same breast. Their fathers passed away early in life. Their mother remarried six times. She was soft-spoken and no great beauty, but men did not last; the women outlived them all. I've never met my grandmother. The only glimpses I've seen of her are through photos of a small, frail woman, with folds of wrinkles and milky eyes. She was nearly blind by the end of her life.

My auntie is the only family my mother has left.

If you want to know about my life, go and speak with Tais before it is too late, my mother says.

My auntie lives with her son's family in St. Paul. She is elderly; in a word, she is dying. She asked my mother to come visit before the fog of old age sets in completely. In these moments of clarity, which grow fewer and farther between, she had things to say while she was still able. They spent the day together; my mother cooked for her older sister and sat with her on faded couches in the living room.

I asked my mother how she was handling her older sister succumbing to age. There were no tears in her voice, only a quiet resignation.

Because I was the younger sister, I could never love her as much as she loved me.

As the youngest of eleven, I understand the love between siblings that echoes throughout generations. My eldest sister and I paid our auntie a visit so we could hear our mother's stories.

When my mother was small, her older sister was already a young woman. My auntie married into the Vang clan. My father's clan. My auntie had married one of his cousins. My father was a man in his late twenties. He already had a wife and a son when he learned that his cousin's new wife had a younger sister. He journeyed through jungles to steal my mother as his second wife. At thirteen years old, my mother was more girl than woman. She walked alone along a dirt road to the farm when my father found her. She tried to fight him off. She cried, kicked, and screamed. My grandmother was out killing two chickens for supper.

When my mother speaks of my grandmother, whose home she was taken from too early, she gazes into the distance.

You don't know how lucky you are.

At her wedding, my mother tried to stab my father with a utensil. Donned in traditional Hmong clothes with heavy layers, she pulled off the winding wraps around her body to make it easier to run away and slipped down a hill. She was caught again. My father sent for a small silver helicopter from the General to take them to what would become her new home, days away from her village. She had never seen an aircraft before, and even though she hated my father, had thrashed and spit like a feral cat up till this point, she clutched him the entire way, scared to death at this alien contraption lifting them into the air. The pilot remarked how affectionate she seemed toward her new husband. Once their feet touched the earth, she released my father immediately and propelled herself as far away from him as possible. My father's house was not far from his cousin's, where my auntie waited. After they landed, my mother ran past her new residence and straight into her older sister's arms.

My auntie recalled standing in the doorway of her home.

I saw your mother run to me crying. She was just a child. She had not even developed breasts yet when your father took her.

When my mother stepped into the role of second wife, she entered an intricate labyrinth of power balances. My father's first wife ran the household. My mother learned to tread carefully and not overstep her. Whenever my mother walked past, the first wife spat at her feet and left a gob of dribble on the floor. The first wife often pushed my father's patience. She threw hot water on him once, and he grabbed her by the hair, dragging her outside to beat her. For all the fight my mother had put up at the beginning of their marriage, she understood my father was not to be crossed.

My father gave my mother piles of his laundry to wash. She walked to and from the well every day. The water jostled on her small back and splashed all over her. She went to her older sister and said she had no extra clothes to change into. My auntie sewed together pieces of fabric to make garments for her.

My mother's in-laws treated her with kindness and loved her like a daughter. When the first wife wasn't looking, her father-in-law snuck her leftovers from his own bowl, saying aloud to no one in particular that he could not finish it. When the husbands went away for the day, beyond the hill to carry out their work for the General, the young wives in the neighborhood gathered outside to play under the sun, skipping rope. One day my mother saw my father walking down the side of the mountain in his uniform. From the threshold of their home, she watched the light of the fading sun move behind him. She had always cleaned and mended his clothes with the utmost care; she would eventually learn to care for him, too.

When my mother became pregnant with my eldest brother, she craved bitter greens, which her in-laws gathered for her. In the coming months, she watched her once-flat midsection balloon in size. I imagine her peering down at her swollen stomach. She strokes the mound of her belly, the skin taut like a drum.

My mother gave birth in a room alone. My father came in only once to brace her as she pushed. There were no doctors or drugs to ease her pain. She did not know if she would survive. She did not fear for her own life. Instead, she was afraid if she died, no one would love her child. She murmured words to my eldest brother and summoned everything inside of her and pushed.

After I gave birth, I was so happy to be alive, I didn't have time to be sad.

My mother spent whole days walking around with Leng wrapped to her chest or resting upon her back. I picture a slight teenager, bent at an angle, pacing in the dusty grass, cooing over her baby. Her will for survival transformed into a fierce love for her children.

As I sit cross-legged on the carpeted floor, between the pair of sisters who have grown old together—the elder with thinning hair and missing teeth, and the younger with long black hair in a bun and weathered hands—my auntie says, *There is no one like your mother. I think I'm pretty good,* she chuckles and starts to cough, *but your mother,* she pauses, *your mother loves everyone. She is good down to her soul.*

While our family grew, so did whispers of a communist takeover. War was at hand. My father uprooted our family to Ban Vinai. He sent my mother and eldest siblings first, along with his son from the first wife to accompany her. Each day, crowds would gather at the airstrip in Long Tieng in hopes of fleeing across the border. I see a rush of wind blowing my mother's hair into her eyes, pieces of her clothing swirling all around her. These planes did not have steps for passengers to gracefully ascend; with all the strength he possessed, my father grabbed my mother, pregnant with my eldest sister, and lifted her into the air, throwing her aboard the aircraft. The first wife was left behind.

Lining the walls of my parents' home in south Minneapolis are framed photos stacked side by side or on top of one another. There is a black-and-white photograph of my mother taken right before she came to America. I can't tell what she is feeling in this picture. My mother is a lot like the *Mona Lisa* in that way. Her expression, if not fully guarded, conceals something. The stern beauty. She has the look of all immigrants in old-timey portraits, standing stiff and straight. There is no smile to ease the intensity or directness of her stare. Garbed in a traditional black shirt and pants with thick neon green and pink cloth wound tight around her waist, her shape is hard to make out. She has always been a small woman. Maybe in her early twenties at the time, she had given birth to four children already. Trails of heavy silver trinkets fan out across her chest and neck.

As a young girl, I would look upon the photo and marvel at the beauty she possessed, hoping I, too, would come into my own one day. Her hair is hidden, tucked into a dark purple turban with a pinstripe X on the front. Her face is bare and unadorned. With clear skin and high cheekbones, she was beautiful to the bone. She has a mole above her left eye, beneath the arch of her brow, which is said to be a sign of good luck. Her wide lips, the top one slightly fuller than the bottom, and pronounced cupid's bow are traits my sisters and I inherited. I see my older sisters in her; growing up, I saw very little of me. People say that I resemble my mother very much. Perhaps it is in our smile, the way our eyes crinkle and our faces light up. If I am like my mother in appearance, in her resilience and capacity to love, I consider it my sign of luck.

Gao Vang earned her master of fine arts in creative writing at the University of Minnesota. She is a nonfiction writer born and raised in south Minneapolis with wanderlust in her heart. She is working on a Hmong American family memoir about the indelible bond between siblings and navigating liminal spaces of love and grief. This essay is dedicated to her mother, and all Hmong mothers, who bear the strength and dignity of multitudes.

Running Away

Mai Neng Moua

"What should I do with my car?" the woman asked in Hmong.

Blong and I were at a gas station on Highway 55 in Golden Valley, where the woman had called us from a pay phone and asked us to pick her up. She was standing outside a rusted Toyota minivan. Her hair was pulled back into a ponytail. In the yellow light of the gas station, she looked thin and pale. She was probably tired from the three-hour drive from southwest Minnesota. In her mid-twenties, she was a few years younger than me but looked haggard. The blank eyes of two little kids—a boy and a girl—stared at us from the minivan.

"Should I leave it at the hotel?" asked the woman.

Earlier when I had asked Blong about the car, he'd said, "We don't need to worry about it," as if the woman had taken care of it.

Blong and I didn't know this woman. We were doing a favor for Ka, a good friend of his aunt. Ka couldn't help her because she lived in Texas. Ka told us the woman's husband was abusing her and she was planning to run away with her two kids while he was at work. Ka wanted us to help her find a hotel for the night and a cab to the airport the next day. She told us the woman had bought one-way tickets to California.

"Maybe I can call him tonight and tell him to pick up the car tomorrow after we leave," suggested the woman.

"You should call him when you get to California," I said quickly. "If you call him now, he might not let you leave."

"Could I leave my car at your house?" asked the woman.

Clearly, she had not thought this through. I looked at Blong since he was the one who hadn't wanted to consider the car situation earlier. "What do you think we should do?" I asked.

"Ah, you could leave it at the hotel," stuttered Blong. "I-I guess you could leave it at our house."

Blong and I stood there, looking at the woman. *What did we get ourselves into?* I wondered. It was 2007, and we'd been married for four years. We didn't have any kids yet. Although my friend didn't believe there was domestic violence in the Hmong community because it didn't happen in his family, here was an example of a Hmong woman whose husband was beating her. I thought about the girl I taught in Sunday School whom I met years later to find bruises on her upper arm where a hand had gripped her, hard. "You know," she said, as if I knew what it was like to be abused, too. "No, I don't," I'd told her. "You know it's not normal, right?" She didn't answer me.

I thought about Blong's cousin who came to him for help divorcing her husband, who had beaten her multiple times in front of her two little kids. Like a good girl, she had gone to his relatives for help. They'd counseled him to be better. But they couldn't stop him from beating her. She was on her own. Having exhausted the Hmong channels, she came to Blong for help using the American court system to divorce her husband. While we waited for Blong to finish up the paperwork, she asked, "Does your husband beat you, too?" I thought she was joking so I laughed. Then I saw the look on her face. She was serious. "No. My husband doesn't beat me."

"Could you drive my car to your house?" asked the woman, looking at me.

"Oh, you drive it," I said.

"I don't like driving in the big cities. There are always a lot of cars."

"Oh, you'll be okay," I reassured her. She had, after all, driven the three hours here. "There are no cars now," I said. It was 9 PM. "Our house is not too far from here. It's just this highway, and then small streets all the way there."

The woman got in her minivan and followed us to our house in North Minneapolis.

"What do we call you?" Blong asked the woman. We were driving toward the airport to get the woman a hotel room.

"Aalia," answered the woman from the back seat, where she was sitting with her two kids.

An unusual name for a traditional Hmong woman, I thought. *Did her parents give her that name?* Or was she like the Hmong kids in the eighties who gave themselves American names such as Stacey or Tony so they could fit in? Or maybe she was like the Hmong college students in Thailand who adopted Thai names so Thai people would accept them. It was probably more that Hmong people loved Bollywood movies. You didn't need to understand the language to know what was going on. Aalia was probably the protagonist in one of the Bollywood movies the woman watched.

"Do you have a Hmong name?" asked Blong.

"Mai," answered the woman.

Every Hmong woman is a *Mai*, which means "beloved" or "dear daughter."

"Mai," I said, choosing to call her Mai since it was a generic Hmong woman's name, and, in a way, it protected her identity. "Do you have neej tsa here?"

Neej tsa is the Hmong word for relatives from her side of the family. These were the people who could exert pressure on her husband's side of the family to exert pressure on him to treat her right.

"My aunt has a son in St. Paul. But most of my people are in California."

In the Hmong community, a wife running away from her husband, even if it is to escape domestic violence, is called a *nkauj fa*. This is translated as a married woman who runs away or divorces her husband. She initiates the actions. And that is the cause of the negative connotation. One online Hmong-English dictionary even translated *nkauj fa* as "adulteress." I'm not sure about that translation, but clearly the word indicates something wrong, bad, or evil. If you helped a nkauj fa, you could get in trouble. It was almost like you were harboring a criminal. I was not surprised Mai had not gone to her cousin for help.

"When did you come to the United States?" asked Blong, breaking my train of thought.

"I came in 1995," answered the woman.

I did the math quickly in my head. She was maybe thirteen years old. *Nineteen ninety-five was the year I graduated from college.*

"Where did you live when you came?" continued Blong.
"I lived in North Carolina."
"When did you marry?"
"I married in 1996."
"When did you move to southwest Minnesota?"
"1997."
"Did you live in Minneapolis or St. Paul before moving there?"
"No. My husband and I moved from North Carolina straight there."

I didn't know anyone in southwest Minnesota, but I had heard that, in the early 1990s, some Hmong families started moving there. The Hmong were credited with saving one of those small towns.

"Do you and your husband come to Minneapolis and St. Paul much?" asked Blong.

"Yes, we come to St. Paul to buy things for our gas station. We've been to the flea markets on White Bear and the one on Como."

Blong and I had been to both Hmong flea markets. We'd stopped by the Aldrich Arena market once before going to hit some golf balls at the driving range next door. The flea market was full of cheap toys and trinkets, bras that were too big for any Hmong woman, carousels of polyester pants and flowered shirts. In the summer, Hmong Town on Como Avenue had an outdoor flea market full of home-grown vegetables, dried herbal medicine, and handmade Hmong clothes. It also had two buildings with small stalls of vendors selling music, books, and Southeast Asian fare. The deli area had its side doors propped open and the fans on full blast, but they only circulated the heat of the mid-July air. It felt like a flea market in Laos or Thailand, not St. Paul.

"When you return the car," continued Mai, "take it to the parking lot on White Bear and he can come pick it up."

"Okay," I said. "Please call and let us know when you want us to do it. Call us first and then call him, okay?"

Although I wanted to stick around to see the man who got off on beating his wife, Blong didn't care to. "Why?" he asked, not wanting to make things any more personal. I wasn't sure why. Maybe it was because I wanted to know if he was like my cousin who didn't stay home to help his two wives with their five kids but instead went out to play soccer or cards, drink beer, and flirt with girls. Or was he more like my uncle who had cut open his wife's head when he flung a plate at her? Uncle and Aunt lived across the hall from us in the fourplex in Frogtown in St. Paul. Late one night, my aunt rushed into our apartment, her head bleeding. I called 9-1-1. My mom told me to ride with her in the ambulance. I stayed by her side in the emergency room. I saw the white of her skull. I saw the broken shrapnel embedded in the tissue. I was in tenth grade.

My uncle spent some time in jail. My aunt became a nkauj fa and took her baby with her to her parents' house. My relatives all said she ran away. The gossip was that her parents told her to do it. It was their meddling ways that caused the divorce, not my uncle's abuse. For some reason, it was too far outside the realm of possibilities for my aunt to divorce my uncle on her own. The event scared me. I didn't want to marry a Hmong man because I was afraid that might happen to me, too.

Mai nodded in response to my request to call us first. The car was quiet as each of us gathered our own thoughts. I prayed for an open hotel room near the airport. It was a couple days before the Fourth of July weekend. Several of the hotels were fully booked when I checked online earlier. One or two were still open, but I couldn't reserve a room since I didn't know how many kids Mai had and what kind of room she wanted.

"Do you think my husband can take money out of our bank account?" asked Mai.

"Yes, he can take money out of the account just like you," said Blong.

"Did you take money out before you left?" I asked.

"I took out a little bit," said Mai. "Do you think there's a bank open now?"

"What's your bank?" I asked.

"Wells Fargo."

"Oh, we can stop at a machine," said Blong. "That's not a problem."

"I don't have a card."

"Oh! How do you take money out?" I asked.

"I go in and give them my ID."

"There's no bank open now," said Blong. It was about 9:30 PM.

"Oh, really?" sighed Mai.

Why had she not taken out all the money? I wondered. I didn't know what time her husband worked, but couldn't she have taken it out after he left for work and before the bank closed? It made me mad that she was so unprepared. I decided to change the subject.

"Mai, what time does your plane leave tomorrow?" I asked.

"Six-fifty in the morning."

"Okay, when do you get to Sacramento?"

"Eight in the evening."

"Really? Why is it going to take so long to get there?"

All I could think about was how Mai's husband was going to come home in the morning and find his family gone. He was going to go straight to the bank and take out all the money. And there was nothing she could do about it.

"I don't know. I bought the tickets through a Hmong travel agency."

Mai's comment reminded me of last year's trip to Thailand, a few days before Christmas. I'd called one of the Hmong travel agencies, thinking that since they regularly booked trips to Thailand, they'd be able to give me the best deals on tickets. One of the agents told me that there were absolutely no flights to Thailand during the holidays. We had to travel later—in January, he said. "No, thanks!" I said. I found my own tickets online. Why hadn't Mai gone online to find her own tickets? She seemed to be at the mercy of everyone, including the Hmong travel agent who sold her one-way tickets that took all day.

"Mai, have you gone to the kwv tij?" I asked, wanting to know if she'd exhausted the Hmong channels of relief.

"No, I have not."

I was surprised by her answer. A Hmong woman who had trouble with her husband was supposed to go to the designated uncle from her husband's side of the family, who had been assigned to help her at the traditional Hmong marriage ceremony. Instead of going to the kwv tij first, she was going straight to her neej tsa in California. It was a bold move for a Hmong woman to involve her side of the family immediately.

"My husband won't listen to them. If he doesn't listen to them, it's not going to do any good."

I nodded in agreement. "Mai, are you sure you want to divorce him?" I asked. I had to ask.

"Yes."

"Are you sure your parents will let you divorce him? What if they force you to go back to him?"

Hmong parents did not like divorce. As if the failed marriage were their fault (they didn't raise a good girl), they often wanted to save the marriage despite abuse or infidelity. That is why parents sometimes forced their daughters to go back to their husbands to try harder, to be more patient, to not talk back—as if it were the women's fault their husbands cheated on them or beat them up. In my mother-in-law's case, when my father-in-law cheated on her, she was told to "follow him, go wherever he goes," as if this were going to stop him from cheating on her again.

"If I don't want to come back, I don't think they'll force me to."

"Okay. But you must be strong and bear through it," I said.

Mai nodded in understanding. "I don't care about anything else, but we have a small gas station. Can he do something with it?"

"Sure," said Blong. "He can give it away. He can sell it. He can close it up."

"Really?" sighed Mai.

"Mai, this is the van that will take you to the airport. It leaves every hour, so you have to be here at five o'clock in order to make your six-fifty flight, okay?" I said.

Mai and I were standing in front of the hotel doors, looking at the airport shuttle. We'd spent what seemed like the whole night looking for a room.

"Don't forget! It's free. You don't have to pay for it. You tell the driver the airline, and he'll drop you off right in the front, okay?"

Mai nodded. Blong and I decided to book the room under my name and pay for it with my credit card. That way no one could find Mai or trace her activities. She paid us in cash. We helped Mai and her kids take their luggage up to their room. Blong called the receptionist and asked for a wake-up call at 4 AM.

"Mai, Blong asked them to wake you up at four in the morning. Is that too early?" I asked.

"No, that's okay."

"Okay. When the phone rings, that's them calling to wake you up."

Mai nodded. "Thank you both so much for your help. I don't know what I would've done without you. Thank you."

"It's nothing. It's okay," said Blong. He took out one of his business cards. "This is my phone number. Call if there's anything."

"We better give her my number since you're going to be in court tomorrow," I said. I took Blong's business card and wrote my name and number on the back. I handed it to Mai. "Mai, Blong's going to be busy tomorrow, so call me. This is my cell phone."

"Thank you. Thank you for helping me."

"It's nothing. Be well. Good luck," I said.

"Call us when you get to California," repeated Blong.

Mai nodded.

"Get some sleep," suggested Blong.

As we left the hotel, I breathed a heavy sigh of relief. Blong and I had driven up and down I-494 looking for a room. I was sweating from getting in and out of the car, running to a hotel's front desk, only to run back to the car and drive to the next hotel. I worried that we wouldn't find a room. It wasn't that I didn't want to help. I did, but I was not prepared to have Mai and her kids stay at my house or drive them to the airport at 5 AM. That had not been part of the deal. Neither was keeping Mai's minivan in our garage. I was not prepared to have Mai's husband know where we lived. I didn't want any bullets in the mail or who knew what else could happen with an angry Hmong man. We finally found a room in the last hotel on my list.

At 4:50 AM, my cell phone rang. I was tired and didn't pick up the phone. And then I realized: it was Mai calling me! As I jumped out of bed and fumbled through my bag for the list of hotels to call her back, Blong's cell phone rang. I picked it up.

"Aunt Mai Neng, I'm so worried," said Mai. Her voice sounded small and far away.

"What happened?" I asked.

"I called him last night, and he didn't pick up. Maybe I should go back home and try it later," suggested Mai. "Please tell me what to do. What should I do?"

"Well, if you go back now, what if he's madder at you? You've already spent money on the tickets to California. You've come this far. I think you should go to California."

"Oh, the shuttle's here. I have to go!"

"Oh, okay."

"Could I keep my car at your house until I figure out what to do about it?"

"Sure, sure. Don't worry about it. Just get on the shuttle."

"Okay, bye."

"Bye."

I sat on the couch, fully awake now. I shook my head and hoped that Mai and her kids were on their way to California.

When Mai did not call after a couple days, I suggested we call Ka in Texas. Maybe Mai had called her to let her know that she'd made it to California.

"No! Who cares? She has our number. She'll call us when she wants," said Blong.

I wondered how he could be so nonchalant about the whole thing. Did he really not care? But I remembered that before we married, he had helped a cousin move out of her husband's house. His two housemates, who were from the same clan, had not helped her. They didn't want to get in trouble. Four days after Mai left for California, Blong's cell phone rang. I picked it up since he was still asleep.

"May I speak with Blong Yang, please?" asked a woman in Hmong.

"He's not available right now. I'm his wife; you may speak with me."

"I'm Mai's older sister. She called and told me to come and get her minivan," said the woman.

"She did?" I asked. Mai had not mentioned an older sister when I asked her if she had family in Minnesota. "Did she get to California? We never heard from her."

"Yes, she got to California. She said she's coming back Monday. I don't know if it's this Monday or next Monday. She wanted me to pick up her car."

"Well, it can't be today. We have some guests over."

We had cousins from Wisconsin staying with us for the big Fourth of July soccer tournament at McMurray Field in St. Paul. This was the annual outdoor festival that brought thousands of Hmong from around the country to Minnesota. It featured Hmong teams competing in soccer, volleyball, and other sports. Vendors sold grilled food on the side of a steep hill; it was a feat to walk the length of its forty-five-degree incline.

"Maybe tomorrow? Could you call back then?"

"Sure," said the woman.

"What's your name?" I asked.

"Niam Tou," said the woman.

It shouldn't have surprised me that she introduced herself as "Mother" Tou, which was really Mrs. Tou or Tou's wife. It reminded me of when I accompanied Blong to a speaking engagement in Wisconsin and a young Hmong woman introduced herself as "Niam Pheng." I stared at her name tag, expecting something along the lines of Amy Yang or Mai Neng Moua, but instead saw "Niam Pheng." She thought I couldn't read Hmong.

"You know!" she said. "Pheng's wife."

She wasn't wrong. Hmong tradition dictated that everyone in her husband's family called her "Daughter-in-Law Pheng," "Pheng's Wife," or "Mrs. Pheng." And like her, I was never just Mai Neng Moua. Blong's side of the family always called me "Nyab Blong" (Daughter-in-Law Blong) or "Niam Tij Blong" (Wife of Older Brother Blong) or "Niam Blong" (Mrs. Blong).

Niam Tou did not call back on Monday as she said she would. She didn't call back on Tuesday or Wednesday, either. Like Blong, I shrugged it off. Everything was strange so far; Niam Tou fit right into the mix. Thursday evening as Blong and I were making dinner, Blong's cell phone rang. He answered the phone. It was Mai. He put her on speakerphone so we both could hear her.

"I'm back at the airport," said Mai. "I'd like to come and pick up the minivan. Could you give my older sister directions to your house?"

She does have an older sister! I thought. The older sister got on the phone.

"There's a gas station on Penn and Twenty-Sixth. We could meet there," suggested Blong.

"I know a gas station on Broadway right off 94. Could we meet there instead?" asked the older sister.

"Sure, I know where that is. We'll meet you there," said Blong.

Blong drove Mai's minivan while I drove our car to the Beehive (Old Colony) on Washington Avenue right off 94. He parked Mai's van on the street. We waited outside our car and soon spotted another Camry driving up to the gas station. Mai got out of the car and walked toward us.

"Hey, don't you know that lady?" asked Blong, pointing to the older sister, who was filling up the Camry at the pump.

I looked more closely. The older sister, or Niam Tou, turned out to be Ann from my mom's church. Her husband, Tou, was a close friend of my older brother. Hmong tradition dictated that I call Ann's mom "Grandmother" since she was married to my "Grandfather," our clan leader who had died in Thailand. Ann and I were part of the same extended family who went to the same church and attended the same weddings and funerals. I walked over to Ann.

"Hey, I didn't know it was you!" I said.

"I didn't know it was you, either!" Ann responded. "Mai said Mai Neng Yang married to a Blong Yang, a lawyer in Minneapolis. I thought it might've been you. I didn't think you'd changed your name."

"I didn't. It's still Mai Neng Moua. She probably thought it was Mai Neng Yang because Blong's a Yang. So, how are you related to Mai?"

"Mai's father and my mother are brother and sister."

"Wow. You're first cousins!"

Only in the Hmong community could this happen. I had no idea I'd be related to Mai, the woman who I thought was just the friend of Ka, who was the friend of Blong's aunt. Mai, the woman who lived three hours away in southwest Minnesota and who was being beaten by her husband, was related to me by one degree of separation.

"What's going to happen now?" I asked.

"Her husband's really mad at her and won't let her back into the house."

"Well, it's probably not a good idea for them to go back, then. If he's that mad, he could hurt her, and none of us will be there to stop him."

"They're going to stay at my house for now," responded Ann. "I didn't even know she was leaving him until she called me from California. I wish she had told me. I could've given her some advice."

I remembered that Ann had been divorced before she married her current husband. She came into the marriage with two young kids, whom her husband adopted.

"So what's going to happen now?" I asked again.

"The kwv tij and neej tsa will call a meeting and try to resolve things," said Ann.

"Why did she go back?" I asked Blong.

"I don't know. Don't worry. She'll be fine," said Blong. "She's got plenty of people helping her."

"I hope so," I said. "She just seems so lost, y'know."

Was Mai the type of person who couldn't make her own decisions, so she'd ask a hundred people for advice? Or perhaps that was just a way to get sympathy? Or maybe she really did know what she wanted but just needed the support to go through it.

A week later, Blong received two phone calls from Texas: one from Ka and one from his aunt. Both wanted to know what Mai could do. We didn't know if the kwv tij–neej tsa meeting ever took place, and if it did, we had no idea how things went.

"There's nothing anyone can do for her now," stated Blong. "If she wants to divorce him, she needs to hire an attorney and pay her to take care of it soon."

They both wanted to know how much it would cost.

"This isn't going to be an easy one. I'd say anywhere in the ballpark of five to ten thousand dollars."

They both thought that was a lot of money.

"Look, tell Mai to call me. She's got my card."

Mai never called. We never heard from her again.

Mai Neng Moua is a writer spinning tales of what it means to be Hmong in America. Her memoir, The Bride Price: A Hmong Wedding Story, *was published in 2017. She is the founder of* Paj Ntaub Voice Hmoob Literary Journal *and editor of the first Hmong American anthology,* Bamboo Among the Oaks: Contemporary Writing by Hmong Americans. *Her artistic awards include the Bush Artist Fellowship, the Minnesota State Arts Board Artist Initiative Grant, the Jerome Foundation Travel Grant, the Loft Literary Center's Mentor Series, and Kundiman's Creative Nonfiction Intensive. Mai Neng lives in Minneapolis with her husband and two girls.*

My Sister Is Depressed

Maly Vang

I can no longer watch you use my sister.
I can no longer sit here and see you make her cry.
I can no longer hear stories about you.
I can no longer let this shit get by.

My sister is depressed.
She wakes up every morning and pretends that she is fine.
She goes to work, comes home and takes care of the kids,
    cooks and cleans, and gives her children baths.
She doesn't ask for help.
She doesn't complain, but trust me, she is depressed.

After her showers, she'll look in the mirror and grab the
    three-inch tire around her waist.
She'll put her arms out and shake her underarms—just to let
    it all hang out.
She can see the cellulite on her thighs and the dark bags
    under her eyes.
She doesn't ask for help.
She doesn't complain, but trust me, she is depressed.

She just lost a child.
She is bleeding.
She is aching.
Her body hurts.
Her heart is broken.
And for a split second or so, she is no longer a mom, a wife, a
    woman, or herself.
She goes to work, comes home and takes care of the kids,
    cooks and cleans, and gives her children baths.

She doesn't ask for help.
She doesn't complain, but trust me, she is depressed.

She looks through your phone.
She sees the messages.
She reads the texts.
She looks down at herself and sees the three-inch tire sitting
    on her lap.
Too afraid to say anything.
Too afraid to ask why.
Too afraid to answer the why.
But she doesn't ask for help.
She doesn't complain, but trust me, she is depressed.

She cries herself to sleep every night.
She grew old.
She grew ugly.
She is not as pretty as she used to be.
And she is not as free as she used to be.
So many responsibilities.
So many thoughts of just leaving everything behind.
So
many
times
she
felt
alone.
Fake laughs.
Fake smiles.
Fake stories just to make them happy.
She doesn't ask for help.
She doesn't complain, but trust me, she's depressed.

You tell her to not believe their stories.
You tell her it's gonna be okay.
You tell her to wait.
You tell her that you love her.
You tell her that you care.

You know. . . .
Sometimes actions speak louder than words.
Have you hugged her?
Wiped away her tears?
Did you hold her?
Comfort her?

You love the fact that she would clean and cook for you.
You love the fact that you could hurt her and she would stay.
You love the fact that you could do what you want to her and
    she would still love you the same.
My sister asked for help.
My sister did complain.
My sister is no longer depressed.

*Maly Vang is a mother, sister, friend, and woman from Milwaukee,
Wisconsin, whose creative drive is beyond measure. With a strong
focus on family and coming together as a unit, Maly writes from
the heart in hopes to connect and heal. A mother of five and a sister
of nine, she puts her values and faith in family first.*

Daughter Poem

Talee Vang

Daughter
Speak with a delicate tongue
So that words will drip from your lips
And send the boys running
Bucket in hand, ready to capture every syllable

Daughter
Rise with the sun
And dance in the steam of rice, cooking in the morning
Greet your new mother and father with
A gentle smile as they criticize the texture of your work

Daughter
Be like the blue ocean water
Flow with your husband's demands
Trickle down the multiple paths carved out for you
And cleanse your household with your purity

Daughter
Be like the cold earth's mud
Mold your dreams, desires, and hunger after your husband's
And live in harmony, unified and supported

Daughter
Learn to love your new family
More than you love your old
For when time stops and your body is laid to rest
You will belong with them

Daughter
Keep your skin soft as dough
But grow your heart to be as fierce as a tiger
When you learn to accept these things
Strength will become of you

Daughter
Laugh when you are hurt
Bite your tongue when you are angry
Be strong when you feel weak
And let no one look into your eyes

Daughter
Be subservient
Remain silent
Follow others
Work hard
Be strong
Love unconditionally
Forgive others
Quiet your soul
Kill your dreams
Live for your children
See but don't speak
Feel but don't cry
Fear but don't run!

For I cannot protect you

And if you don't listen to these words of wisdom
The world will fight you
They will rip your spirit apart
And I cannot be there to comfort you
And I cannot bear your sorrow
And I cannot heal your wounds
And I cannot erase the pain
And I just want your life to be
As easy and simple as possible

Daughter
One day, when you have children of your own,
Maybe you will understand . . .

Momma
Thank you for your love and concern
I will find my way
I am courageous, strong, and resilient because of you

Kuv niam
Be assured that I will bring you honor and joy

Talee Vang *started writing and performing poetry in high school,
using spoken word as a tool to combat injustice in society. Her passion for underserved populations stems from her lived experiences.
She has traveled throughout the Midwest performing and teaching spoken word. Talee is daughter, sister, wife, nyab, mother to
four beautiful children, and a doctor of psychology. She advocates
for womanism as opposed to feminism because she believes that
Hmong women should stand united with—rather than divided
from—their brothers.*

PART 3

Grand (Mothers) We Love

The Grandmothers We Love

Boonmee Yang

In a world where many suffer in silence, let us not forget the grandmothers we love. They are such complex creatures. Yet only after their ghosts are left do many of us fully realize this.

As a child, I divided people into two simple categories: Kind or Unkind. For example, my mom was Kind because she'd always blow on the forkful of coiled pho noodles before feeding me. Mrs. Kjeldseth, however, was Unkind. She called me by a different name throughout the third grade, despite multiple corrections.

My *pog* was an exception. She moved between both categories as if they were separated by a permeable membrane. I was raised mainly under her care, which complicated how we behaved as grandmother and grandson. Kind Pog periodically took me to the corner grocery store to purchase the two-for-one generic Oreo sandwich cookies with her colorful food stamps. Kind Pog showed me how delicious sliced white bread tasted when dipped into heavily sugared instant Folgers coffee.

Unkind Pog was addicted to nagging. Unkind Pog tattled on us to my dad when he'd come home to a messy living room. Most importantly, Unkind Pog was the antithesis to my childhood energy. We loved each other, but liking one another was optional. With her, I never got to be a child. Add in the complexity of being the firstborn son in a Hmong family (though I was the sixth child): she expected me to model maturity for my younger brothers from age three. She held me accountable for activities I believed little children should be free to do: jump, run, build forts with the sofa cushions, and climb everything. My younger brothers and I couldn't do these things inside the house, nor could we play outside for long, due to her paranoia about kidnappings. For her, I was always older, even when I was only starting kindergarten.

Across the yard, though, resided the kind of grandmother for which I yearned. Nestled inside my neighbor's duplex was a grandmother who allowed me to freely be a child. She didn't punish me for being too loud or messy. Her greetings included a smile and a butterscotch wrapped in crinkly, golden cellophane paper. She also had a bamboo bong that never left her side. Despite the opium addiction, I put her under Kind.

(I'd known what a bong was from having been raised around other elderly Hmong who had opium addictions when my family lived in the projects in West St. Paul. Opium addiction was a secret that all the children in the neighborhood knew about but no adults spoke of.)

She had two grandsons, whom she doted on. Daniel (not his actual name) was a chubby Hmong boy with a bowl cut. Like me, he was also starting kindergarten. His older brother, H. Seng, was not like most boys I'd met.

My initial encounter with H. Seng ended with me screaming. His most striking features were the burn scars that plagued his body. His outer ears had burned off, leaving only the canal openings. His hair was desert vegetation: sparse, thin, and wispy. His bottom lip fused into his chin, revealing some of his lower teeth. Both his hands had been amputated; his grandmother would attach special dining utensils for him to use during meals. He would joke about how he felt like Captain Hook when wearing them.

I spent many afternoons in Daniel's living room. While we jumped on sofa cushions, ate junk food, and chased one another, his grandmother sat out back in the three-season porch to get high. Yet, never did I feel unsafe. When it was time to go home, I'd slowly walk down the stairs, wishing Daniel and I could switch grandmothers.

One day, I finally asked about his older brother. Daniel shared that before he was born, their grandmother had left H. Seng behind to go grocery shopping. She'd also forgotten a pot of water boiling on the stove. The apartment caught on fire, and, too little to reach the doorknob, H. Seng was trapped inside.

When my family relocated to St. Paul that summer, I was more sad about leaving Daniel's grandmother than I was about leaving my Minneapolis friends.

Years later, I picked up a local newspaper and saw a familiar scarred boy with wiry black hair on the front page. The center-fold featured him holding up an incredibly detailed sketching of the White House. Mentioned in the article was also an insight that Daniel had left out: their grandmother was high when she left the apartment on that fateful day

In that moment, truth, perspective, and age came together for a jarring revelation. The fire was no accident. It was careless-ness. I recall wondering: How does a family live with an addict who almost killed their child? Why did she not give up her habit after the fire? Did H. Seng forgive her, and how? All those years of yearning for a grandmother like her, it never occurred to me that, to someone else, she may have been their Unkind.

But I had also begun to understand the complex relationship between opium and my people. Much like my *pog,* opium couldn't be rigidly labeled. As deadly as the addiction was, many Hmong gardeners, like my mom, still planted opium poppies because the vibrant flowers reminded them of their homeland. Though countless infants lost their lives to opium overdoses during the escape from Laos, its cultivation also provided income to sustain families.

After finishing the article, I looked over to my *pog,* who had begun spending her days staring silently out the kitchen window. I'd grown quieter as well, especially after my dad died. Perhaps, like me, she'd decided that keeping her thoughts private was eas-ier than trying to explain her feelings to others. That afternoon, I realized how little I knew about the woman who'd spent more than a decade raising me. For someone who'd spoken frequently during my childhood, rarely had any of her words been about herself.

As an adult, I'd like to believe my system of cataloging peo-ple has developed some complexity. I can now understand my *pog* and Daniel's grandmother as more than just either/or. Both women were war survivors whom I'd tried to simplify.

Like other Hmong grandmothers, effects of the war left my

pog and Daniel's grandmother aching for an impossible healing. During an era when many Hmong families were displaced
throughout the world, abiding by the Refugee Code to survive
didn't afford us time to slow down and examine war trauma,
let alone try to create a word for PTSD in our language. Both
women learned to cope without self-help books. Whereas Daniel's grandmother found solitary refuge in the hollow of her bamboo bong, my *pog*'s coping mechanism manifested itself as an
overly protective, fierce-loving woman who repressed the war
terrors she'd witnessed in order to spare me from them. It is no
small feat to swallow years of trauma to the very last gulp of air
on one's deathbed.

Like our people, both women were flowers ripped out of their
ancestors' gardens and thrust into foreign soil, leaving behind
tangled roots. Here, at the mercy of white-gloved hands, they
were directed to flourish among flowers that feared them as an
invasive species. With our roots having grown forty years strong
and three generations deep, perhaps now we can afford to linger
a moment. May it be used to remember the grandmothers we
love, freed from the restraints of labels.

*Boonmee Yang often turns to writing to avoid completing other
responsibilities, including writing itself. He has hundreds of half-
finished stories saved as drafts on his old Myspace account that he
would like to (but no longer can) access, as well as on his Tumblr,
Facebook Notes, and Macbook that will likely never see satisfactory conclusions, much like life itself. His author crush is Viet
Thanh Nguyen.*

The Chicken in the Airport

MaiThao Xiong

My mom used to say, "*Peb ruam ruam*," meaning "We are stupid," to describe herself and my father. At the time, I wasn't aware that she didn't mean this literally—it was her way to motivate us to work harder than her and to be more than she could be. Her encouragement and love are not expressed through her words but through her actions—and, of course, through food.

A few years ago, we arrived exhausted at Denver International Airport to visit one of my sisters. My older sister, Vai, was busy keeping track of her four- and five-year-olds, Madelyn and Adam, both restless and jubilant after their first-ever airplane ride. Panou, MaiYang, and MaiVue—my other sisters—directed their attention to complaining about our ride being late. My younger brother, Chong, the only adult male on the trip, sat outside of our circle, thumbs attacking a phone screen.

As we sat waiting, Mom pulled a lump of aluminum foil the size of a soccer ball from the plastic bag that she had stowed into her carry-on backpack. Slowly, she peeled back the layers of foil, revealing the center of the lump—a white, unchopped, full-sized, boiled chicken, seasoned in black pepper and salt. The aroma of moist meat permeated the arrival area.

"*Nej puas noj?*" "Do you want to eat?" she asked loudly. Non-Hmong passengers arriving from baggage claim slowed down and cast glances toward the Hmong woman in a leopard-print blouse and black dress pants that clashed with tennis shoes and a fake leather cross-body purse, fat protruding like a pregnant woman's belly, waving the naked chicken at our faces. Tall, smartly dressed men and women hurried away from our group of eight spread out across the floor, smelling like chicken. But Mom wasn't concerned with anything but her chicken and the thought of feeding her children.

"*Nej puas noj?*" Mom asked again. We shook our heads no to eating boiled chicken at the airport.

"Suit yourself," Mom said. Her hands, wrinkled and calloused from too many hours in the garden, tore a leg from the chicken. A satisfying snap of the bones. She grinned. "Mmm, so good."

I don't know why I felt self-conscious to eat Hmong food in that public space. I had learned to embrace my Hmong American identity, but I guess Denver was not like Minnesota, where most folks knew about Hmong people and our foods. Maybe it was the day—people had been staring at our group, the flight took longer than expected, it was 4 PM and we had not eaten since 10 AM, our ride was late, people were *still* staring at us. And there was Mom, who had casually packed a full boiled chicken for a two-hour flight.

Mom, whose own mother passed away when she was a young girl, took care of her siblings until she married. She, along with my father, was a slash-and-burn farmer with land and livestock in Laos but fled due to threats of Hmong genocide after the Vietnam War in 1975. She was pregnant with her first child at the time. Later, she came to America with my father, my five older sisters, and me in 1992. Whenever things went wrong, she relied on what she knew in order to survive a situation. She always packed boiled chicken to travel because that was the food she could rely on.

I realized my mother was used to this process because she had flown by herself many times. She was able to navigate airports without knowing how to read or speak a single word of English. And she knew the pitfalls of traveling: it drains energy, and if you don't know how to order food in that country, you starved. If you did manage to order, you might struggle with the price. It was much like that when she first arrived in America.

At the Denver International Airport, even when we refused her offer, we watched the boiled chicken. The first leg found its way into the hands of Madelyn, who took it without a second thought. Another snap, and Mom shoved a leg into Adam's palms. His teeth shredded the meat, lips smacking in satisfaction. Keeping her eyes on her children's reactions, Mom said, "I also brought *kua txob*," producing a snack-size Ziploc bag packed with a red and yellow Thai pepper sauce that had been ground and seasoned with salt, lime juice, and fish sauce.

That was when we gave in.

Vai fetched her children and ushered them to the bathroom across the hall to wash their hands. Nou, MaiYang, and MaiVue abandoned their conversation, my brother joined the group, and we assured each other that we would only eat a little because Mom had already pulled it out and we didn't want her to feel bad for eating alone. We sped to the bathroom, washed our hands, and raced back. All five of my siblings, hands vigorously traveling from all directions, dismembered Mom's boiled chicken. As the meat was furiously stripped from every bone, Mom laughed. She passed out purple sticky rice, already packaged in individual, snack-sized Ziploc bags. She couldn't stop grinning, amused at her stupid children for refusing a meal when they were starving. "I thought you guys didn't want to eat?"

I had grown up on the taste of plain, boiled, organic chicken dipped in Thai pepper sauce. Living away from home for the last two years, I'd been eating frozen Tyson chicken strips without the pepper sauce. There's a joke in the family—and maybe among other Hmong families, too—that lazy people don't have freshly ground Thai pepper sauce because it's a dish you have to put a lot of effort into. First you have to use a mortar and pestle to smash the peppers. Then it requires little amounts of ingredients— garlic, lime juice, salt, sugar, and whatever other seasonings— that, added carefully, make a big difference. The cleanup can burn your eyes if you are sensitive to the sting of pepper, and the essence of garlic pulp remains on your fingertips for days.

I smeared breast meat with Thai pepper sauce. It tasted like heaven.

It reminded me of when I was nineteen and I studied abroad in Seoul, South Korea. Before I left, Mom bought some beef jerky from an Asian grocery store and tucked it into my check-in luggage, also stuffing a plastic bag loaded with sticky rice wrapped in banana leaves into my carry-on. I thought it was a bother and unnecessary because I imagined that after I arrived I would be grilling barbecue beef and slurping on kimchi jjigae. I traveled with four other classmates and carried the stench of the banana leaves and sticky rice onto the twenty-hour flight. I didn't dare open my bag because doing so would contaminate the airplane with the sweet, overly ripened banana smell. My classmates and I became separated in Seoul, resulting in a whole afternoon searching for each other. By the time we finally regrouped, most shops were closed. The few that were open didn't have menus, and we didn't know how to ask for food. That evening, starving at our hostel, I unpacked Mom's smelly sticky rice and rubbery beef jerky to share with the group. My travel companions squealed with excitement upon seeing the food and asked whose smart idea it was to have brought it. I ballooned with pride and said, "My mother."

That day at the Denver airport, I swelled with the same pride. The frustration and fatigue had melted away with each bite of chicken. I don't know how Mom had the time to boil a chicken, make the pepper sauce, and steam fresh sticky rice—enough for eight travelers—all within the morning before the flight. She's resilient and unapologetically herself. I can't imagine why I believed her when she called herself stupid.

MaiThao Xiong is a writer in St. Paul, Minnesota. She was born in Ban Vinai refugee camp in Thailand and moved to Minnesota with her family of nine when she was a year old. She graduated from St. Catherine University with a bachelor of arts in English and communication studies. She wrote and collected stories for nonprofits, including Mary's Pence and Prepare + Prosper. She is currently pursuing a master of fine arts in writing at Augsburg College.

In Her Death, My Mother Came to Life

Linda Vang Kim

She Was My Mother

Our son, Elliot, was born on January 3, 2017. Only about a week later my mother, Chia, passed away. As Elliot continues to age, adding first days and months and, later, years to his life, I will be reminded of the days, months, and years since my mother has left us.

When she was alive, I never fully understood the degree to which she made sacrifices for our family. Perhaps as children we take for granted the love a mother gives without asking for or taking anything in return. I incorrectly believed a mom does what she does because she *has* to. She works tirelessly into the night while her children sleep soundly because she *must*. Plus she is *superhuman* anyway and incapable of having the usual emotions the rest of us do, feelings such as fear, frustration, and fatigue. These beliefs kept my view of her simplistic—she existed to take care of me and would not spare any expense or effort because to me she had an abundance of both.

However, at her funeral and in conversations with my siblings after her death, I finally began to see her complexity and dimensionality. Ironically, in her death my mother came to life.

I could finally imagine that she, too, probably got tired after working twelve grueling hours in the hot sun (but never showed it). She, too, was probably scared of taking public transit in a foreign country where she did not speak the language (but remained calm so that her children would as well). This realization, much too late, gave me great sadness, knowing she probably felt many of these emotions in isolation. While it is too late for me to ask, *Mom, why are you sad?* or *Mom, are you tired?* I want to remember my mother for her leadership as the fierce matriarch of our family.

Among her greatest attributes, my mother was resilient, fear-less, resourceful and hardworking, and generous.

She Was Resilient

Chia lost her mother at a young age, around eight years old I am told, and so was thrust prematurely into adulthood. Unable to fully and adequately grieve the loss of her mother, she was ex-pected to welcome her new stepmother into the family soon af-ter. As the eldest in her family, she also carried the heavy burden of caring for her younger siblings. This early painful experience must have helped grow and fuel her inner fight. This fight would serve her well as throughout her life my mother had several se-rious medical emergencies, yet she survived them all. She never gave in or relented in even the most hopeless and dire situations.

One summer, as a day laborer for a local farmer, she was rid-ing in the vehicle that transported workers to the field when it got involved in a serious car accident. I remember visiting her in the hospital after her surgery and seeing the four-inch scar in the shape of an elongated "C" on the right side of her face, stretching from forehead to cheek. To a twelve-year old, the stitches seemed to be all that was holding her face from splitting apart. Luckily, she made a full recovery, and the lingering "C" on the side of her face was the only reminder of that fearful day.

A few years later, she was diagnosed with breast cancer. Choosing to forego chemotherapy treatment, she opted instead to remove her left breast. Post-mastectomy, she always seemed to hide her entire left side behind others when posing for photos. Yet, at that time I never imagined she would or could have been self-conscious. Believing so would have reduced her to a level of vanity I simply did not believe mothers were capable of having.

In 2008, she suffered an aneurysm that required extensive brain surgery, six months of rehabilitation in the hospital, and years of recovery at home. The first days after she was admitted to the ICU, both close and distant relatives visited her and us in the hospital. Many returned to the waiting area after viewing her, shaking their heads vigorously in disbelief. Most had already resigned hope and immediately got to work convincing us (her children) that "pulling the plug" was a viable option when even her doctors had not yet considered this. Much to everyone's surprise, she survived this episode as well, and we had our mom for another nine years. In this extra time she got to see me get married, complete my master's degree, and bring three children into this world.

She Was Fearless

She had a difficult marriage, arranged by the fathers of two people who could not have been farther from being in love. As a result, she described instances where she often parented alone, which meant there was no room for fear and doubt.

One story she frequently told during the last two years of her life happened back in Laos. She would recall this story especially during the times my two daughters accompanied me on a visit to see her. They were the same ages as my two older sisters were at the time the story took place, so seeing my girls seemed to transport Mom back as if it was yesterday.

One day when she was returning from her family's field, she had an extremely close call with a tiger. Before continuing with the story, she would point out that my father was not with her, as usual, so the lives of her two young children lay solely in her hands. Xyo, my oldest sister, was sitting on the back of their horse while my mother carried Maika on her back. The horse was secured by a rope around its neck, which my mother held onto tightly. However, the horse became spooked by a wild animal (my mom believed it was a tiger) and broke free. It bucked my sister off its back and took off running down the path in the opposite direction. Frantically, my mother caught up to the horse and returned to find Xyo in the ditch calling out, "Kuv niam, kuv poob tom nom lawm-os!" After securing Xyo back up on the horse, my mother quickened her pace, her radar for danger operating at maximum strength for the duration of the trip.

Many years later, in America, my mother would demonstrate her fearlessness many times over. In one instance, she mastered the city's public transit system even in the time before there was

Google or the internet. In the early 1980s, Asian grocery stores were few and far between, so we traveled the extra distance from the east side of St. Paul to the Midway area to buy rice. We did not own a car, so low rice supply in our house meant the four of us younger children would tag along with my mother to catch the bus bound for Kim's Grocery on Snelling Avenue. How she managed to navigate the transit system without speaking or reading English remains a mystery to me. If she was fearful, she never showed it; as a child, I found these trips to be a great adventure and I never feared for my safety or security. What a sight it must have been for the driver pulling up to the bus stop to let a mother and her four young children board with a very large bag of rice and multiple gallons of milk.

She Was Resourceful and Hardworking

Growing up, I knew we were poor, but I never worried about an empty stomach or having a warm bed to sleep in. Sure, we lived in the projects and received food stamps, but the miracles my mother performed in stretching her limited income meant we received the things we needed and often even the things we wanted. This is a testament to her resourcefulness and hard work, and when it came to her children these skills especially seemed to kick into super high gear.

When my sister Xy graduated from high school, my mom threw her a graduation party like many parents do. The difference in this party was how she managed to negotiate with local Asian grocery store owners to provide supplies needed on credit. She did not postpone or delay the celebration until the government assistance she heavily relied on paid out on its own inconvenient schedule. That my mother pulled it all together quietly and discreetly represented her selflessness in never expecting or wanting recognition for the things she did. Her own happiness seemed tightly bound to the happiness of her children.

Whether it was moments of celebration or times of difficulty, we could rely on our mother to come through for us. Believing education was the ticket for her children to escape poverty, she supported each and every one of us who went off to college. When my older brother Kageh found himself short by several thousand dollars when his tuition bill came due one semester, my mother did not let pride keep her from calling every relative in her phone book. She only stopped when someone agreed to give my brother a loan to cover the difference so he could continue his studies.

She also used her agricultural knowledge and skills to secure summer income opportunities such as picking cucumbers for the Gedney Corporation and selling vegetables at the St. Paul Farmers' Market. While two-parent households boasted extra earning potential and support of each other, my mother had legally (not just culturally) divorced my father by that time, and so she seemed to compensate by working twice as long and twice as hard. Working alongside her, I tired easily and was frustrated by the amount of manual labor we had to endure. It was especially difficult when I knew many of my classmates spent their summers traveling, going to camp, playing with friends, and riding bikes around their neighborhood. Yet, I never imagined then that my mother would feel the same sense of tiredness and yearning for an easier and more leisurely way of life.

She Was Generous

Above all else, my mother was generous. My fondest memory is triggered by vanilla ice cream, the kind that comes in the large plastic gallon container. Whenever we went grocery shopping, my mother always let us pick out our favorite foods. She may have been tightening her wallet all the while but never told us "no" as we took turns grabbing our favorite treats from the shelves and throwing them into the shopping cart. My favorite treat was vanilla ice cream, and because our family was big, we had to buy the gallon size. As soon as we got home, I would volunteer to scoop out the ice cream into cones and pass them out to my family. I always gave my mom the first cone and served myself the last, yet she would eat hers so slowly (or I inhaled mine so quickly) that we would end up in a stare down. I must have been salivating as I watched my mother eat her cone, because inevitably, without any words, she would extend it in my direction. I would be so happy to savor this second helping of ice cream. She never hesitated in giving to her children the things they most desired or wished for.

For all seventy-eight years of her life, my mother exemplified unparalleled leadership by loving deeply and unconditionally. She succeeded in taking care of her family despite her humble means. Though she is no longer with us, she will never be forgotten.

*Born and raised in St. Paul, Minnesota, **Linda Vang Kim** is mother to Lucy, Eunice, and Elliot and partner to Yong. She is a graduate of St. Paul Central High School, Carleton College, and the University of Minnesota. Linda works as an academic adviser in the College of Education and Human Development at the University of Minnesota Twin Cities.*

On Father's Day

Nou Yang

On Father's Day, I am reminded that it was a woman who raised me. A woman who had to go into battles alone.

Battles of survival:

growing up as an orphan

raising five children to adulthood and losing two;

living in the jungle; and

crossing the Mekong.

Battles of navigating newness:

starting over in a strange land;

driving a car you once only dreamed of;

supporting the educational aspirations of your children in a system you have never gone through;

learning a foreign language;

raising a challenging Hmong American teenager; and

balancing both Hmong and Western cultures as the head of household.

On Father's Day, I am reminded of the burdens she had to carry
alone:

> to be responsible for every action of her children;

> to carry the weight of my reputation—the Hmong com-
> munity would judge my mom's ability to raise us based on
> my behavior.

On Father's Day, I am reminded that the Hmong community values men more than women.

> I am reminded that the Hmong community does not place
> such burdens on men, whether or not they are present.

> I am reminded of how people used to make me feel "less
> than"—that I would grow up to be a "mi nyuam laib" (bad
> rebellious child) because I lacked a father figure or male
> authority.

> I am reminded of my brothers and male cousins who
> stepped in and took on the role of father figure and tried
> to provide guidance.

On Father's Day, I am reminded that I am not fatherless. Rather,
my mother and father are one and the same.

On Father's Day, I am reminded that my mother is enough just
as she is . . . full of

> strength,

> courage,

> bravery,

> fierce independence,

purpose,

capacity, and

resilience.

Kuv niam, I love you on Mother's Day, but perhaps it is on Father's Day that I love you even more.

Nou Yang is passionate about creating spaces for collaborative learning and dialogue around issues of identity, cross-cultural leadership, youth development, and gender equity. Her twenty years of professional experience include direct service work, fostering leadership opportunities, and engaging community toward action and management. A Hmong refugee, Nou believes deeply that all people have value and that growth happens through reflection, listening, and dialogue. Nou is an alumna of the Marshall Memorial Fellowship, a leadership program that fosters connections between the United States and Europe to build transatlantic leaders; and a past board member of Hnub Tshiab: Hmong Women Achieving Together.

Pure Love

Douachee Vang

Kaj Ntshiab and her niam were grocery shopping at the Hmong store. It was there that Kaj Ntshiab realized, once again, that some of her aunts and uncles who were shopping were giving them strange looks. She saw that they whispered to one another and kept giving Kaj Ntshiab and her niam side glances. When they got closer to each relative, they were given a simple greeting before being quickly abandoned. Kaj Ntshiab looked at her niam when she interacted with the relatives and saw how she remained relaxed, smiled, and spoke with a calm tone.

When they arrived home, the sun had already hid itself halfway under the horizon, coloring the sky with a wash of pink and orange. Kaj Ntshiab and her niam unloaded the car and put the groceries in the fridge where her artwork, grades, and notes were pinned with magnets. While Kaj Ntshiab did her homework on the dinner table, her niam made her favorite pork stir-fry and a batch of steamed white rice. Kaj Ntshiab could smell the earthy scent of fresh cilantro and green onion mixed with ginger and garlic, along with the aroma of jasmine rice filling the kitchen. For Kaj Ntshiab, time passed too quickly when she and her niam were at home, especially when it was nighttime; as soon as dinner was set and eaten, it was already time to get ready for bed.

After washing the dishes with her niam, Kaj Ntshiab took a shower, brushed her teeth, and ran to her bedroom and jumped into bed: she was ready to sleep in for the weekend. Like every other night, Kaj Ntshiab's niam peeked into her room to check up on her. That was when Kaj Ntshiab mustered up some courage to ask her niam a question.

"Niam—why do some of our aunts and uncles look at us funny whenever they see us?"

Instead of ignoring the topic, Kaj Ntshiab's niam walked over to the bed and tucked herself in. She then replied while giving Kaj Ntshiab a gentle hug, "It's just because they don't understand my love for you."

"But," Kaj Ntshiab continued, "isn't it because we left Txiv? I heard the other kids talk about it, and it makes me sad and confused."

Kaj Ntshiab's niam sat in silence while still holding her daughter, thinking about how to approach the subject. Finally, her niam said, "Have I ever told you the story of your niam tais?"

"No," Kaj Ntshiab answered, curious as to what her niam had in mind.

Kaj Ntshiab's niam moved around to get more comfortable. "Well, then, it looks like I have the perfect bedtime story and history lesson for you."

"Okay!" Kaj Ntshiab answered excitedly.

Kaj Ntshiab's niam cleared her throat and began.

"Puag thaum ub, your niam tais came from a place called Laos in Southeast Asia. She and I were running away from a dangerous place; at that time, I was about the same age as you—eight. The two of us ran through a big jungle for many days and many nights. But we weren't the only ones—a lot of other families were also with us. We were all trying to reach the Mekong River at the edge of the jungle so that we could cross it and make it into the safety of Thailand. After countless days and nights of tirelessly running, we all finally reached the river. We jumped in and swam as fast as we could across the river. Many people didn't make it across, but for those who did, we eventually made it to Thailand.

"After spending a few months in Thailand, your niam tais and I were able to get a sponsor from America. Now, a sponsor in this situation is someone who is willing to pay, support, and care for another family to live in a new place and start a new life. So, when this sponsor helped your niam tais and me, we both flew to America in a big airplane. While on the plane, your niam tais and I heard stories about how America was all white: there were only white people, and the land and trees and anything that we could possibly imagine in America was white."

"Really?" Kaj Ntshiab exclaimed, puzzled. "That's funny. Why did Niam Tais and you think that?"

"Because," Kaj Ntshiab's niam explained, "everyone back in Laos used to make stories about Americans being white, so people just believed in it since we didn't know what was the truth. But not only that, elders made stories that Americans ate other humans—that they were cannibals!"

Kaj Ntshiab shivered from fear and grabbed onto her niam. "That's scary!" Kaj Ntshiab's niam held her closer for comfort and assurance, chuckled, and then kissed the top of Kaj Ntshiab's head. "It's okay; it was just a lie that they told us. There is no such thing as people eating other people. Many of the elders only said this so that we Hmong people would stay in Laos and not flee to America."

Kaj Ntshiab released her grip and asked, "And then?"

"The funny thing is," Kaj Ntshiab's niam continued, "when Niam Tais and I arrived to America, we really thought that it was all white like how the elders had described. It was snowing at that time, and all the snow covered the trees and the ground and the buildings. We were scared and thought that maybe the elders in Laos were telling the truth after all. But luckily our sponsor and a translator told us that it was just snow."

Kaj Ntshiab's niam continued with, "I remember when I was in fourth grade, a girl came up to me and told me to go back to my country because America wasn't our home."

Kaj Ntshiab responded, "Why? That's mean. Did you cry?"

"They just didn't understand who the Hmong people were," her niam said with a reassuring smile. "But don't worry; I didn't cry. I remember looking back at the girl and telling her what I had just learned in school: that America was not her land, either, and that it was the Native Americans' land to begin with. After that, she didn't say anything else to me."

Kaj Ntshiab giggled.

"I also remember that I didn't like shoes because I never wore shoes in Laos. That's why even today I don't really like to wear high heels and would rather be barefoot most of the time. But even though I didn't like shoes, I loved getting new clothes from the Salvation Army and other charities. I was always excited when it was time to get new clothes because I never had so many outfits before. But other than that, it was hard at home because I had to help Niam Tais with all of the chores since it was just me and her in our family."

After hearing this, Kaj Ntshiab started to wonder about Yawm Txiv. "Niam," Kaj Ntshiab questioned, "what about Yawm Txiv? You haven't said anything about him."

Kaj Ntshiab's niam went quiet for a while. Then she said, "Your niam tais left your yawm txiv a long time ago before you were born, and because of that, everyone kind of ignored her and didn't talk to her much or, worse, they would talk behind her back."

Kaj Ntshiab waited for her niam to continue speaking, but she saw that Niam was looking at the teal-colored wall, lost in thought. Finally, still looking off into the distance, her niam continued, "In our culture, it is never right for a woman to leave her husband. She is just supposed to 'ua siab ntev.' If a woman does leave, it will make her become a 'bad woman' to everyone else because she couldn't stay and keep the family together."

After some somber silence, Kaj Ntshiab's niam said confidently, "But you know what?"

"What?" Kaj Ntshiab replied with a smile.

"Don't be afraid by what our Hmong culture and other people say or think. Having a family with only one parent is not a bad thing, like everyone keeps saying. I have you, and as long as we have each other we can make it through anything. Besides, Niam Tais was able to do it alone with just me and her, and thanks to Niam Tais's hard work of raising me up I now have a brave, smart, and beautiful daughter like you. You are the best thing to happen to me, and I don't regret any of it. No matter what anyone says, Kaj Ntshiab, just remember this: don't let them intimidate you—don't let them make decisions for you or pressure you into staying in one place or situation forever. There is such a big world out there that you can discover, and you can do anything and everything that you desire if you put your mind to it."

Kaj Ntshiab's niam gave her one more tight squeeze and kissed her forehead.

Kaj Ntshiab hugged her niam some more and closed her eyes. It was very late now, and Kaj Ntshiab's eyes were getting heavier and heavier, just as the stars and moon outside grew brighter and larger. Kaj Ntshiab quickly drifted off into sleep, and after some time, her niam slowly untucked herself from the bed. She pulled the covers up to tuck in Kaj Ntshiab and then knelt beside her bed, gently moving the hair from Kaj Ntshiab's face.

"Good night, my sweet daughter, kuv mi nplooj siab Kaj Ntshiab. May your life always be full of purity and joy just like your name."

Douachee Vang *majored in women's studies at Fresno State and was a Ronald E. McNair Scholar and a Michigan Humanities Emerging Research Scholar. She will complete her master's in cultural studies at the University of Washington Bothell in spring 2020. Douachee is passionate about feminism, power and knowledge, and social media studies/activism. She hopes to contribute more/critical Hmong studies scholarship into academia and her community. In her free time, Douachee can be found watching YouTube or Netflix and, more importantly, writing her feelings out. Her written work has appeared in zines and small anthologies. She is actively learning and unlearning, dismantling, and surviving.*

My Grandma Can Freestyle

Tou SaiKo Lee

This was the first night that Grandma Zuag Tsab (pronounced *Zhua Cha*), who had arrived to the United States from Laos several years prior, came to see me perform spoken word poetry. She walked with a hint of a limp that, she later explained, came from pieces of shrapnel lodged in her left leg from a land mine left behind after the Secret War many years ago. Dad had to guess her age when doing paperwork to sponsor her over to this country since she was born in a village during a time when Hmong were not required to document birth dates. At this community event at Harding High School in St. Paul, I planned to perform a piece about my journey to find cultural identity.

The host announced: "Next to the stage is a guy who grew up on the east side and is going to perform spoken words for us. Give it up for Tou SaiKo Lee!"

I stepped center stage and adjusted the mic stand to right underneath my bottom lip. "Yeah . . . first of all, for *spoken word* there is no need for an *s* after *word*. Thank you for inviting me to perform. I also grew up in Frogtown, where I made a lot of hip-hop songs with my brother; then we moved to the east side for a bunch of years; now I do spoken word, too. This poem is called 'Generation after generation.'"

I projected: "Generation after generation, we've been warned by the OGs, lost in what is, who we are . . ."

Those of us who were raised in the United States refer to Hmong elders as "OGs," which stands for Older Generation. While I spoke through poetry, I squinted at the bright intensity high up from across the room and noticed rocking shadows in seats of the auditorium. I felt like I needed to take out my trusty sunglasses from a pocket and rock it inside the building to block

99

out the shine—and to perform with my eyes closed without anyone knowing. Ha!

I continued to articulate: "I'll admit that my second tongue
has been eclipsing my first since birth or since first grade, and
I've been slowly trying to get it back"

I heard snaps, claps, and foot taps from students in the first
few rows. I began losing my native language when I started going to school. Now, I spoke Hmong at the level of a small child. I
started relearning my language right after high school.

"The fate of our culture depends on our future. Educating
our youth to acknowledge and embrace their roots. Support the
cause, the struggle, the shining life force. Our culture is immor-
tal. Generation after generation," blared out of the speakers.

After the applause, I leaned over to murmur, "Thank you, *Ua
Tsaug.*"

I removed my shades and strolled backstage toward Grandma
while she waved to me. She was wearing the furry snow leopard
hat I gave her as a gift last December. Mom scolded me about why
I would buy Grandma something meant for teenagers. Grandma
had worn the stuffed animal over her head since that day and
never complained.

Grandma laughed deeply and heartily, like Santa. I noticed
that she laughed a lot—and not always when something was
funny. She laughed when my dad yelled at her for saying inap-
propriate words around us children. She laughed after surviving a car accident during which she swears all passengers were
protected by a special ring on her middle finger. She laughed at
the flat-screen TV when the Rock hit Mankind with a metal fold-
ing chair while in the wrestling ring. Some get offended by her
laughing at awkward moments, but I understand. I do that, too.

She said, *"Tub, kuv tsis paub xyov koj hais dabtsi hauv lus aakis,
tabsis zoo li koj ua tib yam li kuv ua."* Tou, I don't know what you
said in English, but it seems like what you do is just like what I do.

My parents mentioned to us that Grandma does *kwv txhiaj*, a
traditional art of poetry chanting that Hmong have been doing
for generations, since we were in China, before the mass exodus.

During 1854–73, many of our people in the southern provinces left in protest of persecution from an oppressive dynasty to nurture villages among the mountains of Southeast Asia. These poems were passed on to her from relatives and still include ancient words influenced by Hmong Chinese dialects. I remember as a teen experiencing an elder on stage performing *kwv txhiaj* at the RiverCentre during Hmong New Year. I never really understood this arts tradition that the OGs do. I hadn't felt like I could relate to it—until the moment Grandma said those words to me after my performance. I realized that spoken word could be a continuation of an oral tradition. What I do in spoken word can honor what she does with *kwv txhiaj*. It would be epic to collaborate with Grandma!

I dropped by my parents' house the next day, darted through rooms, and rehearsed what I was going to say, since speaking Hmong was no longer natural to me. I knocked on Grandma's bedroom door. She tapped on my shoulder from the kitchen behind me. I shifted sideways to see her.

I asked, *"Pog, koj puas kam hais koj cov kwv txhiaj nrog kuv cov paj huam Meskas es peb ua yeej yam ua ke?"* Grandma, would you be willing to say your *kwv txhiaj* with my American poetry to perform together?

She responded, *"Koj hais qhov chaws nyob twg ces, kuv ma li nyob ntawv hais kwv txhiaj."* You tell me where the place is, and I will be there ready to perform *kwv txhiaj*.

Pops told me that her generation didn't have the opportunity to go to school; she was a farmer all her life and can't read or write. Even so, she was able to recite poems that were five to ten minutes long by listening and memorizing line by line, stanza by stanza, verse by verse through repetition. Mom informed us that Hmong do *kwv txhiaj* for therapeutic reasons in the middle of a jungle or while they're farming.

Grandma and I sat at the kitchen table to have some of her tofu soup made from soybeans—she got the hookup from her OG friend at an east side farmers' market. She revealed that she has skills to improvise lines that rhyme. Grandma rattled off a

few lines of poetry in Hmong and ended her flow with "St. Paul."
She just gave a shout-out to St. Paul. For sure these lines were not
from Laos. Wow: my grandma can freestyle!

*Tou SaiKo Lee is a spoken word poet, storyteller, hip-hop recording
artist, and community organizer from St. Paul, Minnesota. He has
facilitated songwriting/performance poetry workshops and residencies at schools and community centers in ten US states and in
Thailand. Tou SaiKo received the Jerome Foundation Travel and
Study Grant in 2008, an Intermedia Arts VERVE Spoken Word
grant in 2009, and a Bush Foundation Fellowship in 2016 to utilize
arts to preserve cultural identity. He is writing a memoir about
his collaboration with his grandmother and is working on his first
Hmong-language hip-hop album,* Ntiaj Teb Koom Tes, *which
translates to* Unified Worldwide.

PART 4

Moving through Cultures

My Name Is Hmong

Mainhia Moua

Money Daughter

"It's a long story," I always told people.

When my mom, a Hmong immigrant, gave birth to me in 1994 in small-town Tracy, Minnesota, she intended to name me Mainhia. In Hmong, it is spelled *Maiv Nyiaj*. The prefix *Maiv* is a tender name meaning "daughter." *Nyiaj*, on the other hand, means "money" or "silver." Hmong parents always named their children by certain phrases, and it was like a prophecy to have their children be known by that name or phrase. Since my parents were no longer trapped in the mountains and jungles of Laos and were now in the land of prosperity, they had big goals for their first American-born daughter.

Tracy was home to packaging companies who hired fresh immigrants like my parents. My parents spoke only Hmong. No English. When I was born there, the medical staff did not understand my mom. With no Hmong translators available, the doctors misinterpreted her. Instead, they wrote my name down as *Nhia Mai*, an irregular and unheard-of name in the Hmong culture. Backward.

For the first twenty years of my life, I went by this name. My parents didn't bother changing it because they never had time. When they moved to St. Paul four years after my birth, they worked consistently at their minimum-wage labor jobs, barely able to sacrifice even thirty minutes to eat lunch. Or they were busy trying to connect with their social worker to make sure they met the county's requirements to continue receiving food stamp benefits, WIC vouchers, and discounted Xcel Energy bills. They couldn't find a Hmong translator or lawyer who could help introduce the name-change process to them. It was easier for me to just tell everyone to call me *Mainhia* and ignore what was on the legal documents. Sometimes they'd tell others this funny story about my name and blame it on the faulty American medical system for not doing their jobs correctly.

Mainhia

In elementary school, I hated roll call, especially on the first day of school. I would have to sit patiently in my seat and wait for the teacher to go down the alphabet. When I was in second grade, I went to a public school where it was majority white students. When the teacher did roll call, I started freaking out. When she got to the letter "L," my heart beat a little faster. My turn was coming up next. Little panic attacks set off in my heart, and the rhythm beat louder than the screechy voice she used to call the students' names. Beads of sweat formed on my forehead as the nerves in my brain twitched. My hands shivered and my feet tapped on the floor. My eyes glanced down at the wooden desk.

"Nai-yah May?" the voice screeched.

It happened. I perked my head up and slowly raised my right hand in the air.

I didn't bother to correct her. Instead, I said, "You can call me Mainhia." I uncrossed my legs and stretched out my foot, pointing at my knee. "'My' like 'my angel' and 'Nhia' like *knee-yah*." I returned my knee under my desk and crossed my legs again. All the students stared at me.

"Wait, so it's flipped around?" she said. "Is there a typo in this sheet?" She lowered her glasses, squinted her eyes, and raised the roll call sheet closer to her face.

My shaky voice responded, "No. Just 'Mainhia.'"

"Well, that's cool!" she said. "I wish I could flip my name like that. How did you come up with that?"

Sigh. "It's a long story," I said to her.

"Nice to have you in my class, Mai nee-hai-ah-ya," she said. "Uh, I'll get it right after a couple more times of practicing." She readjusted her glasses and continued to the next student's name.

In fourth grade, I went to a Hmong charter school. Hmong people can't stay away from other Hmong people. But I was happy because there would be no more white teachers who butchered my name. There would be Hmong teachers this time. I could relate to all the other Hmong students who probably had fancy names like I did. Maybe they were even harder to pronounce than mine.

At least, that's what I thought.

My hopes were quickly dashed. I walked into my classroom, and to my surprise I was greeted by my teacher, a huge white lady. She had a bright smile on her face and blonde hair long enough to cover her broad shoulders. The click of her heels got louder as she walked toward me with a piece of paper in her hand.

"Welcome to fourth grade!" she said in a cheery voice. "What is your name?"

I was shocked. Panic mode. I could use this time to tell her the long story of my name, how my Hmong parents came to America as new immigrants and, at the time of my birth, didn't know how to speak a speck of English and said my name incorrectly to the nurses and doctors in the hospital room, and how I didn't have a say in anything but probably cried a lot, and then the doctors mistakenly wrote my name down as "Nhia Mai" instead of "Mainhia," but the medical staff probably didn't know that "Nhia Mai" is not a proper Hmong name, but they proceeded to write it down anyway while my parents were in the background worried about what would happen to me when the nurses wheeled their baby away—"Honey, what's your name?" the teacher asked again.

My eyes closed. I forgot about everything that just ran through my head. Suddenly, I started tearing up because of how nervous I was.

"Oh, honey, it's okay!" Suddenly, she, this stranger, hugged me. "You'll do just fine; don't worry!" Perhaps she thought I had butterflies in my stomach. She rubbed my head and patted my back. I felt assured, all of my worries gone.

"Now, what is your name, sweetie?" she asked again. This time, she pulled the sheet in front of my face. I looked halfway down the sheet because "N" was located in the middle of the alphabet. Then I saw it and pointed: *Nhia Mai Moua.*

I cleared my throat and got the courage to speak up a little bit. "Please call me 'Mainhia,'" I begged her.

"Mainhia," she said, crisp and clear. "Welcome to fourth grade!"

I was surprised. For the first time, a white person said my name correctly. The tears in my eyes dried up. I was no longer shaking; instead, I looked up to see her beaming, white smile. She told me to go find my seat and put my school supplies in my desk.

My teacher was a great first impression of fourth grade, but everything didn't go as planned. Twenty-four out of twenty-five students in my class were Hmong, but most of them had American names.

"Bao, Bob, Chia, Christopher, Dylan, Fenn, Ger, Her, Jennifer, Ka, Kenny, Lia, Lor—"

Oh no, here we go again. I hope she didn't forget what I told her about my name. The 'Ls' started and I panicked again. Why couldn't my parents give me an American name, like Hannah or Lauren? Chelsea or Melissa? I wouldn't have teachers reminding me of this treacherous birth story. But what if—"Mainhia," she once again called out.

For the first time, it sounded perfect. I had never before heard my name sound so pleasant. It was almost like music to my ears.

I raised my hand and said, "Here." As I looked at her, she winked at me. She smiled at me, and the look on her face assured me that everything was going to be okay.

"What a lovely name, Mainhia," she said. "I'm so happy to have you here." She proceeded to the next student.

Wow, I didn't have to advocate for myself, nor did I need to explain my birth story to her—or anyone else. My name was as easy for her to pronounce as the American-named students in her class. I smiled and lifted up my head for the rest of the roll call.

Mai and Pa

"What is your name?" a skinny Hmong girl asked me later that day during recess. I noticed that she was one of the girls in my classroom.

"Mainhia," I told her.

"That's cool," she said. "My name is Panhia!" Just like the prefix *Mai*, the prefix *Pa* was also common in Hmong girls' names, a term meaning "flower." "Our names are kind of the same!"

"Cool," I said to her. "Do you like your name?"

"Yes, a lot," she told me.

I was shocked. Why did she like her name so much when I was here, begging to be renamed into a simpler, Americanized name? I was curious.

"Why?" I asked her. To my surprise, she answered me in Hmong, but I could understand her clearly because I knew Hmong, too. Many kids my age weren't able to speak Hmong very well.

"Because my parents told me that the Hmong culture is very important to us. We live in America now, but we should be happy that we are Hmong and still have our mom and dad and aunts and uncles and grandpas and grandmas with us."

I knew she had a point, but I didn't understand it at all. I just knew that she had a cheerful and happy attitude all the time. She was extroverted, unlike me, who was always shy and quiet. I figured that in the future, I would probably understand what Panhia just said. Or what her parents said. But for now, all I knew was that I needed to be more like Panhia. Smile, be happy, and go with the flow.

Panhia and I remained great friends for that entire school year. At our Hmong charter school, we learned a lot about the Hmong culture. I remember learning how to recite the Hmong alphabet forward and backward. I remember learning about Hmong back in Laos and Thailand, just like those bedtime stories that my dad used to tell me. Panhia and I talked about the annual Hmong soccer tournament gatherings at McMurray Field and wearing Hmong clothes to the Hmong New Year at the RiverCentre. We also talked about yummy Hmong sausages, papaya salad, sticky rice, and pho. We were getting really geared up on our Hmong knowledge and culture.

All good things come to an end. The next year, she moved away to a new school. The following year, I moved to Maplewood and enrolled in a suburban school. There were no longer Hmong people, but blondies walking around everywhere.

Whitewashing

Living in suburban Minnesota made me forget the Hmong culture. I wanted to be white, like the households on my block that were filled with white people, Cadillacs in their driveways, golden retrievers, and white picket fences. When we walked around the neighborhood, they would stare at our torn-up Goodwill clothing and snicker at us. We would walk with our cheap sandals that were on the verge of snapping apart. We would get stares and complaints because our backyards stank whenever we plucked chicken feathers or burned squirrel fur.

I saw all their stares and heard all their complaints.

"Look at these weird Chinese people."

"They stink."

"They have no manners."

"They are so loud."

I was ashamed. I wasn't Chinese. I was Hmong, but I wanted to blend in with them, not stand out. So I started pressuring my mom to buy poultry from the store, or I'd help her pluck it inside the house; even though our house stank like raw meat, it was better than plucking the chicken outside. I begged my dad not to burn squirrel outside and just buy them skinned from his friends. I tried my best to hide everything inside, literally.

I imitated what white people would do. I forced my mom to buy me Hollister clothing, even though their limited sizes only made my overweight stomach bulge out. I begged my mom to buy me fifty-dollar Converse shoes because they were name brand. Even in eighty-degree weather, I wore them because that's what others wore to look hip. In school, I tried my best to be at the same level as my classmates. Their parents walked out of school with diplomas and degrees in hand and business jobs. Their parents attended their conferences, sporting events, or music festivals. My parents could walk thirty acres (peb caug ev kawj!) to their gardens when they were young. That was their walk.

Hmong parents don't understand why extracurricular activities exist. "Just go to school, come back home, and stay home," says every Hmong parent. But at school, teachers always encouraged everyone to join extracurricular activities. Was I wrong in doing something? Why did I have to act Hmong at home and white at school? Why couldn't I just combine both of them?

Bad Life Like Us

In 2009, my family lost our expensive suburban home to the bank. That following year, my mom came home empty, broken, and distorted; she had just lost her job as a factory packager. My dad had been diagnosed with a physical disability that did not allow him to work.

But they did not tell us children any of this. Mom and Dad told us that we were going to move to a new house, which was not a shocker to us; we always had to move and liked house hunting. At that time, I didn't know that a mice-infested duplex with three bedrooms and one bathroom would have to be enough for our family of seven, but we had no other choice. We would take longer bus rides to school, and during the day, Mom would try her hardest to find a new job with the few skills she had. Luckily, a call came for her six months later, as she found a similar job packaging candles in a warehouse company. Of course, they only paid her minimum wage, and she worked more than forty hours a week, solely standing on her feet.

Mom and Dad still didn't say anything to us. The only thing that came out of their mouths was, "Keep going to school every day so that you won't have a bad life like us."

So every morning, we woke up at 7 AM for school, while Mom had already been at work for two hours by then and Dad was frying eggs and steaming rice for our breakfast.

Hmoob Cob Fab

In 2011, while researching which colleges to apply to the following year, I ran across a disturbing picture. A black-and-white photo of several elderly men in dirty black outfits crouched in a jungle. Their knees rested on the filthy, hard ground that had stones and trash, and children were begging in the background. The men's hands were clasped together and raised up to their chests. Some covered their faces, but most looked straight at the camera. Their eyes squinted as they cried and their mouths frowned.

"Who are these people?" I asked Dad.

"These are the *cob fab* [guerilla soldiers] who are still trapped in the jungles until today," he said.

"What? Why don't they just come out like how you and Mom did?"

"They can't. They're trapped. We were lucky."

This photo bothered me the rest of that day. Who exactly were these people? If they're Hmong, why did they have such sad faces? Why are they not living like my parents in America? Do these people have any significance to me? Is this an outdated photo? How can I reach out to them?

I gave the photo no further thought and instead continued to research colleges. Unfortunately, the photo followed me to my dreams. One night, I saw the same photo, but this time, the man in the center of the photo had the same face as my dad. He was crying, sobbing tears of pain, and his eyes were so squinted that I could barely see them. One hand was pounding the ground; one was pounding his chest.

I woke myself up from this dream, hearing my own sobbing in my sleep. *Thank goodness it was just a dream*, I said to myself. I was drenched in cold sweat. I covered myself with my blanket and slowly fell back asleep, weeping.

I knew I had to get to the bottom of this photo. The next morning, I went to my dad again.

"Dad, who exactly are the *cob fab*, and why are they still in the jungles?"

He proceeded to tell me that other Hmong people were not so lucky. They couldn't escape the concentration camps or cross the Mekong River into Thailand and eventually America. Most of them would spend the rest of their lives under Laotian control, and if the Lao felt like killing them, they could die any second.

I felt horrible. I felt so scared for these people, and my dream made me realize that this could have been my father, or my mother, or my grandparents. I could have been one of the kids begging in the background.

"What can we do to help them?" I asked my dad.

"Keep going to school every day so that you will have the skills to save us Hmong people," Dad said. "Tell them who you really are, and who your people are."

In that moment, I realized my real identity. I am Hmong. Why was I afraid of being Hmong? Why did I shame my name and my identity? I cannot change the fact that I am Hmong. I needed to acknowledge and be okay with my culture. That was the first step in realizing what I need to save my Hmong culture and people.

Angelic Flute

"*Maiv*, come here and listen to my new song."

Dad would always play his *raj* (Hmong flute), this light brown, stained wooden rod that he held up to his lips every day as a means to refresh the ears. I nodded and looked at him, sitting, as always, in his low, bamboo-woven chair. Towering above him, I realized that his hair had grown several white streaks and the wrinkles next to his eyes crinkled deeper. He swished the saliva in his mouth and swallowed it, getting ready to blow his *raj*.

The music echoed throughout the house, as it did every day. But today, it sounded different. It sounded more heartrending. More tragic. More sorrowful. I closed my eyes and saw a scene. In my head, I heard the echoes and cries of the Hmong people in the photo. I saw them in my head, and a helicopter dropped in the jungles of Laos. A girl led the way out of there, followed by an army.

The elderly Hmong people cried, *Koj puas yog Hmoob os*? Are you Hmong?

The girl replied, *Awm kuv yog Hmoob os*. Yes, I am Hmong.

Suddenly, angelic flute music played throughout the jungle, thanks to the girl's majestic discovery, and the Hmong people cried no longer. They all walked together, toward the light, out of the jungle, hands held together. Forward.

Mainhia Moua is a second-generation Hmong American who is passionate about writing, education, and the Hmong culture. Her experience translating between Hmong and English at a young age for her immigrant parents helped her develop an interest in English language and literature; she earned a bachelor of arts degree in English and creative writing from Concordia University, St. Paul. Mainhia has a passion for creative writing, especially about the intergenerational gap between traditional and modern Hmong people; she hopes to write a memoir about this subject one day. Mainhia plans to continue her studies and become an English professor.

The Back of the Line

Dee Kong

My grandmother-in-law, a strong-willed, sassy lady, passed away the afternoon of May 15, 2015. That evening, after working on my philosophy paper, I went to my in-laws' home (my sister and her husband live with his parents) to offer my love and support and to also be there for my nephews. As it typically plays out, the women are bustling around the kitchen preparing dishes and in the dining room setting up the food. The men are seated in the living room, and a few women are seated in the formal living room. Relatives and people from my in-laws' church arrived in a steady rhythm, handing food they brought to the women in the kitchen. They greeted my in-laws with their condolences. The couples separated, the husband to the living room and the wife either to the kitchen or the formal living room.

I entered the home, took off my shoes, paid my respects to my in-laws, and stepped into the kitchen to help my sister. We arranged the numerous plates of food buffet-style on the dining table. After the setup was complete, I headed to the basement, usually the designated kid area, to talk to my fourteen-year-old nephew about his great-grandmother. He shared how he was feeling, how he wished he could have been there for her last moments, and how he already missed his great-grandmother terribly. His face contorted, fighting hard not to cry. He looked down and away—he is a boy, after all, and undoubtedly had been taught "boys don't cry." I tried to reassure him, but he only fought harder to hold back the tears. I said a few words, hoping to comfort him; then we turned our attention to whatever was on the television.

Fifteen minutes later, my sister came downstairs to inform us it was time to eat. As we entered the main floor, we saw that a line of men had formed at the dinner table. My nephew walked over to stand in line. My sister and I remained back to allow the men to get their food first. After most of the men had passed through, the elder women lined up. Still, my sister and I waited until most of the women got their food before we proceeded to the table.

We ate perched on the stairs that led up to the second floor, balancing the plates on our laps. Since we were among the last to get our food, a majority of the people had finished eating. A man walked over to me and my sister and asked, "After you're both finished eating, could you please cover the food on the table?" We instantly set down our plates, obediently did as asked, and returned to our food after we had completed the task. Upon finishing our meal, we picked up around the kitchen. I assigned myself to wash the dishes, and my sister cleaned and tidied up the dining room. After a while, I exited quietly, since I needed to get home to complete schoolwork for class the next day. I know my sister and the women worked and cleaned late into the night.

Women in the kitchen, men in the living room—this is how gender is performed in the Hmong culture, particularly during family or clan-related events. Yet these banal encounters represent and reinforce cultural ideas of gender, particularly that of "Hmong women" and "Hmong men." While I or any of the other women were not explicitly assigned to prepare the food or clean up after everyone, our roles and duties are an unspoken, ingrained expectation. Per usual, there is an exception to this gendered role assignment. At larger family gatherings, where a cow or pig is butchered and prepared for celebrations, it is the men's task to cut the large pieces of meat into smaller sizes, which require their placement in the kitchen or else in the garage. Otherwise, a man in the kitchen, cooking, cleaning, or actively assisting women at such a gathering would be an anomaly.

Mary Talbot in *Language and Gender* states, "discourses are historically constituted bodies of knowledge and practice that shape people, giving positions of power to some but not to others. But they can only exist in social interaction. . . . So discourse

is both action and convention. It is never just one or the other."[1]
Beginning in childhood, Hmong women are taught the roles and
expectations held for them: to be obedient, helpful, quiet, and
subordinate. Many young girls are raised in the kitchen assisting
their mothers. Moreover, Hmong men are taught to be a man, to
hold a man's place at the table, and to represent the family and,
possibly in the future, the clan. During family gatherings, boys
will typically remain in the playroom, some, if slightly older, will
be asked to sit in the living room to learn the customs, while
young girls will be called to help out in the kitchen.

My parents are refugees and immigrated to the United States
in 1979. As the oldest of seven children, I grew up with more traditional practices than those of my younger siblings. When relatives and visitors came over to our home or when we were the
visitors, it was women in the kitchen cooking and cleaning and
men visiting in the living room. The men ate first. After they
finished and left the table, the women and children would eat
what was left. Do not misunderstand: the men did not eat most
of the meal and leave scraps for the women and children. They
made sure there was enough food left, but they had first dibs at
the freshly prepared dishes. Around the age of seven or eight, I
remember thinking how odd it was that the men ate first, but I
didn't question it. My mind also neutralized this oddity because
at home, when it was just my family, we ate together. Furthermore, sometimes the opposite happened: my dad would eat last
or skip meals (I realized when I was older he did this so his seven
kids had enough to eat, as we were very poor). My mom cooked
most of our meals. When my sisters and I were old enough, we
were responsible for cooking for the family.

Daughters were expected to be obedient and to have excel-
lent kitchen skills: chopping meats and vegetables, cooking, and
cleaning so they can be good wives and revered daughters-in-
law. Daughters were also supposed to know when to help and do
things without being asked. My mom hammered these kitchen

---

1. Mary Talbot, *Language and Gender* (Cambridge, UK: Polity Press, 1998),
121.

skills into my sisters and me. When I was five or six, my mom attempted to teach me how to make steamed rice. Left to my own devices after her first instruction, I almost burned down the apartment. She was not pleased at my failure and continued to push me. I successfully made my own pot of steamed rice at the age of seven.

Moreover, daughters-in-law were to be subservient and to work tirelessly and nonstop. If you were a slacking daughter-in-law, the women would talk about your shortcomings and you'd get a "reputation." A good daughter-in-law rises early in the morning to prepare breakfast, assists her mother-in-law in whatever she needs, prepares the meals, takes care of the kids, takes care of her husband, takes care of her in-laws, and cleans. When guests and extended family visit, she hosts, cooks, and cleans for her family and the guests. At large family or clan events, I've witnessed daughters-in-law remain in the kitchen for hours, often eating last or during a quick break.

As immigrants, my parents were not highly educated. They grew up farming in Laos and lived in refugee camps after the Vietnam War. After they immigrated to the United States, they encouraged my siblings and me to study and do well in school to have a better life. My dad worked the graveyard shift for more than thirty years as a janitor, and my mom worked various odd jobs, ending up at a manufacturing company for almost twenty years. As I grew up, my dad encouraged me to be a secretary or teacher. It wasn't because he didn't think I was smart; I excelled in school. Rather, in the early 1980s and 1990s, these were the only jobs he believed most women held. The television shows I remember watching with my parents, *Little House on the Prairie*, *The Dukes of Hazzard*, *Family Ties*, *Knight Rider*, *The Love Boat*, *Gilligan's Island*, and *The Facts of Life*, certainly did not depict women in higher-level, executive positions. Nonetheless, as a result of my elementary and high school education, I learned about women's rights and equalities. I forged an identity and ideals based on the lives of Sojourner Truth, Susan B. Anthony, Maya Angelou, and Rosa Parks and had many strong and encouraging women teachers. Due to the cost, and since we were so poor, I don't believe my parents saw college as a feasible option for me. But I was determined to go to college.

As life happens and forces you to take detours through rough-graveled, deep-potholed, and massively speed-bumped roads, rather than attending college after high school, I completed a two-year legal secretary certificate technical college program. I graduated with distinction in the program and dedicated myself to working hard at the law firm to support my young daughter as well as her father. Through the law firm, I landed a lucrative position that led to financial independence. Despite some personal tumult, at the age of twenty-five I became a homeowner. Financially stable and with my life settling down somewhat, I started my college education. As a single mother, I raised my daughter on the importance of equality, empathy, self-value, independence, feminism, and women's rights. Through my trials, mistakes, and experiences, I released myself from the confines of the traditional expectations held for me. I learned how to embrace my true self. Since I was no longer with my daughter's father, I carried a stigma in the Hmong community. People whispered and spoke about me. Nonetheless, I carried on, and I was proud to be a self-sufficient, independent woman.

Despite being an educated and progressive woman, that evening, as soon as I entered my in-law's home, I fell back into the role of obedient, subservient Hmong woman. As Talbot stated, in this social interaction, a gathering to honor my grandmother-in-law, these are the conventions of women in the kitchen, men in the living room, and men eat first, women second. Everyone at the gathering has an unspoken, ingrained, active role in the performance. These social actions are the discourse that shape us. I automatically went to the kitchen and asked how I could help, started organizing the food, and accepted trays of food from incoming visitors. I've contemplated whether my role in the kitchen and dining room were a sign of respect and to help my in-laws in their loss. Yet, when I am a guest at someone's home, I typically ask how I can help and assert myself somehow.

As progressive as I am, I cannot bring myself to break from these conventions. I cannot explain my reluctance to stand in line with my nephew along with the other men. However, my daughter, who was not present the evening of my grandmother-in-law's passing, would have stood with my nephew. I've seen her beeline it to the front or stand in line with the men at other family gatherings. Maybe one day I will work up the nerve, but for now, I wait my turn at the back of the line.

*Having worked undercover as an eight-to-five office worker, hiding out in Woodbury, Minnesota, **Dee Kong** wandered often in her mind. One day, she took off her orange jumpsuit and escaped to wander the planet. She observes. She reads. She writes. She drinks. She eats. She sleeps. She ponders. She will wander some more.*

the reasons we stand

Boonmee Yang

i fell and
you told me to stand a man
when the only strength i've witnessed
are my mother's and sisters'
who balled their fists against Hunger, swinging
backs bruised, used
as stomping ground for gossip
faces blued from holding their breaths
for help to come along
only to realize they were already here

girl, breathe

they showed me how to dig
nails-into-the-ground-till-they're-in-Chinatown deep;
one naked heel flat against the earth
push up
book-on-your-head back straight
straighter than the world's unbending double standards
head-on-a-platter high, hair-a-mess, chest heaving
look-me-in-the-eye
and tell me

One.
More.
Time.

how you want me to stand a man

Boonmee Yang *often turns to writing to avoid completing other responsibilities, including writing itself. He has hundreds of half-finished stories saved as drafts on his old Myspace account that he would like to (but no longer can) access, as well as on his Tumblr, Facebook Notes, and Macbook that will likely never see satisfactory conclusions, much like life itself. His author crush is Viet Thanh Nguyen.*

Gatekeepers

Kia Moua

Mr. and Mrs. Andersen were the picture-perfect couple. They were quintessential and ideal Methodist Christians. She was simply beautiful, with iridescent pearl-like white skin and soft brunette hair. He was white with a tall, dark, and handsome presence. They were always well dressed and carried themselves accordingly. When they spoke, a bright halo seemed to glow around them, and I would hang on to their every word.

As a child I remember how intently everyone else would listen to them. I envied their ability to capture an audience. They showed me how a "good" person or typical American would act or speak by taking me under their "white" wings of privilege.

I learned I had to assimilate. Something was wrong with me, my family, my race, and my ethnicity if I didn't conform to the norms of this country. As a child, I was mesmerized. I was jealous. I subconsciously internalized how my looks, words, and actions didn't fit that normal mold. No matter how much I went to church and Sunday school, participated in choir and bell choir, I still didn't glow like Mr. and Mrs. Andersen, my childhood mentors/goodwill ambassadors/white saviors.

My family moved to another state where I then had a different mix of nuns, priests, and lay teachers, who continued to colonize my mind. Institutional racism created feelings of embarrassment and stabbed my siblings' egos when the public school counselor stereotyped my National Honor Society brother and sister as English Language Learners. Had this pivotal moment not happened, my path may have had a different outcome.

This experience led my siblings and me to continue our education in private Catholic schools. I was able to learn the ways of the assimilated from the privileged elite. As a senior in high school, I received the Bishops' Award, which basically symbolized the ideal Catholic child. This was purely an example of "who you know," not "what you know." A very small monetary scholarship accompanied the award—which barely paid for one course of books during my freshman year of college.

Upon my high school graduation, I felt ever so eternally grateful and almost embarrassed to see the ten-foot table covered with awards that had my name on them. These "awards" came with no scholarships or grant money, just that good ol' Catholic pride of self-good. (I was more impressed my name was spelled correctly.)

When I attended a local private Catholic college, true colonization revealed itself to me. This college was started by Franciscan nuns, who were responsible for laying the foundation for the college, the local hospital, schools, and churches. They also helped to change their unincorporated township into a major city. (I say this because I believe they were not given the proper credit for all that they did for the community.)

I was fortunate enough to have lay teachers as my religion professors who invited me to question everything I thought I knew to be truth. Religion had been a part of my education since I started fifth grade, so you can imagine what kind of recovery process it takes to heal from the internalized messaging of self, community, government, and what it means to consider myself an "American" when I felt I had never belonged. The movement from the eternal gratitude of a refugee to unpacking my own colonized mind leaves me eternally a refugee.

My faith-community influences, though well intentioned, also stripped me of my heritage. I still don't belong to this country no matter how I've assimilated.

Kia Moua is a Hmong woman born in Laos and now making her home in the Midwest, along with her husband, three girls, and two dogs. Kia is an equity consultant with a passion for social justice in working with individuals and systems. Kia earned a master's degree in human development. In her spare time, she enjoys writing, reading, and exploring the outdoors with family and friends.

PART 5

Breaking Barriers

Roasted Duck

Pa Xiong

People used to ask my mother
why she named me after my aunt,
and she would always say,
so casually,
but so deliberately—
No, no,
I just like the name.

My aunt
who
through the affairs and breakups,
through the threats of fists and bullets
from the angry mouths of no longer
husbands and lovers,
she, my father protected
and
she, my grandmother loved
in spite of.

My aunt
whom
my mother loathed.

She used to visit when we were kids
with her boyfriend-of-the-month
who she would tell us was probably
just temporary,
because that was the way love was—
just temporary.

She always visited with mouth-watering
Peking duck—
such a delicacy
for us little Hmong kids
who didn't get out much.

My mother would caution us each time—
duck tastes good,
but don't eat it too often.
Los los kua muag,
she would say.
It brings so many tears.

My mother
who only knew to be right,
to be good,
who built her self-worth
around the flaws and cracks
of others.

Every time my aunt visited
with her roasted duck
and temporary boyfriend,
I wanted to go home with her.

Pa Xiong is a middle school English teacher living in southern California who holds bachelor's and master's degrees in Asian American studies. She spends most of her time raising her two kids, but here and there, when she can find a moment, she likes to write as well.

Never Again

MayKao Y. Hang

My job was to create a community initiative to prevent violence in the Hmong community at the Amherst H. Wilder Foundation, a nonprofit in St. Paul, Minnesota. It was 1996. I was a young woman with little credibility or social power, and the hiring process had been on standby for a long time. I figured I must not have had the type of qualifications Wilder wanted but was surprised when an offer came. After a year of organizing, *Hmoob Thaj Yeeb* (Hmong Peace) was born, and I had more than a thousand people engaged in violence prevention and intervention activities. As the voices of those impacted by violence rose through me, I became outspoken as an organizer and started receiving hate letters from those who disagreed with the approach I was taking. Ironically, they signed their names. I guess they weren't afraid of a twenty-four-year-old Hmong woman with more heart than sense. It wasn't unusual for me to show up at a community meeting and not be acknowledged, greeted, or given much respect. Yet, I persisted.

I was also a newlywed. My husband, Lao Lu Hang, was raised in rural Michigan in a town of three hundred people. By Hmong norms, we were late to the starting line of life. After defying tradition and beating the odds out of poverty, I had graduated from Brown University and then the Humphrey School of Public Affairs at the University of Minnesota. I could only resist having children until I was twenty-six, and then I caved into the pressure. Having grown up babysitting, the thought of raising children exhausted me. I didn't feel ready to become a parent, having watched my own parents in survival mode—working nonstop to meet our basic needs, and yet never having enough. I never stepped into a movie theater until I was sixteen. Going to McDonald's or Kentucky Fried Chicken was a special treat. Cake and cookies were a luxury we could not afford. I knew children meant responsibility, and I was just starting out in my career.

But the pressure of motherhood came from all corners. And, to my surprise, we conceived right away. At our first ultrasound, we stared at the gray screen to figure out which tiny spots might be the baby. Not a word was said throughout the procedure. Instead, the woman in the crisp white lab coat with efficient movements led us to a small room with a circular table and told us to sit down. A few minutes later, a nurse came in. "I am so sorry. There was no heartbeat, and the fetus isn't viable." I saw that her mouth kept moving, but I really couldn't hear her. I looked at Lu, and his stoic face reflected mine. The nurse told us the "fetus" would discharge soon. Did we want to scrape it out or let it come out naturally?

The self-recriminations began. Was it because I hadn't really wanted a baby and hadn't taken care of myself well enough? I couldn't go into work. My mom came over, made a fuss over straightening up my apartment, and told me every now and then with sympathetic nods that I shouldn't have moved around so much with my usual vigor. I must have scared the spirits, and the baby had detached from me. Three months later, I was still sad and anxious. I hadn't menstruated and wondered if I would be barren. Reading books about miscarriages and stillborn babies had caused fear rather than healing. So I visited the doctor. He made me take a urine test. I was surprised to learn I was four weeks along with another pregnancy. Unlike the first time I was pregnant, I was thrilled. I was so happy; I don't remember feeling tired or sick during the pregnancy. I was excited despite the morning sickness, leg cramps, and lack of air conditioning. The nine months went by fast.

Close to my due date, I picked up a copy of the *St. Paul Pioneer Press* to read at work. I was skimming when I saw a short story reporting the deaths of six Hmong children, all under the age of twelve. Details were sketchy, but the last name of the little children was "Hang," my husband's clan. The youngest who had passed was preschool age, still a baby. I instinctively cradled my round stomach. My baby was supposed to be a boy. I looked up at the cluttered two-person office, gazed out the window, and carefully reread the story. The next day, I picked up the paper again, and there were more details. Oh, my goodness: there were pictures of the children, and a picture of their mother, who had allegedly murdered them. The gruesome details unfolded with controversies around the accuracy of the reporting. Then the request for help came to Wilder. I was a member of the Wilder Community Violence Response Team, and I was asked to find Hmong social workers and mental health workers to debrief and to bring solace to the staff and people at the McDonough Homes Housing Project where the murders had happened.

That day, September 4, 1998, I went into labor but was still calling around to find Hmong social workers who would be willing to help. More details were coming out about the murders, and it was triggering even more grief and horror. I was at home on the sofa, responding to questions from a *Pioneer Press* reporter, when I had to tell him to wait as a contraction came and went. From my two years of organizing, I knew there weren't going to be enough Hmong social workers. From the blood I saw in the toilet that morning, I knew the baby would arrive very soon. I hadn't yet told my husband that I had been having contractions all day. I panicked. My mind became overly active as I imagined the methodic actions of the mother, Khoua Her. Allegedly, the children had been called in from the playground one by one and strangled.

By the time Lu got home from work, the organizing and outreach became a blur of physical and mental pain. This baby was definitely coming. I don't remember how the police were called to McDonough Homes, or who saw what happened first. I felt sorry for the first responders. And now, I don't care about those details anymore. What impacted me was that Khoua Her was the same age as I was. Our two twenty-six-year-old lives intersected to define us both in this moment for eternity. Ironically, I felt our fates could have been interchanged. An odd twist of fate and circumstance had enabled me to become a college-educated Hmong woman while Khoua Her had not been able to—not even close, as we learned much later about her.

My labor went for twenty hours. Almost the entire time, I faded in and out. In my lucid moments, I thought of the children who had been killed by their mother, and then eventually, I felt only the pain and exhaustion of labor. The children were from my husband's clan. I felt they were family, as we are taught from childhood that the clan we marry into would be our permanent home. My dad told me when I married Lu that I had borrowed my mother's womb to be birthed, but that my real mother would be my mother-in-law for life. I objected to what I considered was brainwashing from my dad, but still, I felt loyal to the Hang clan. I had talked to some of Lu's relatives who were worried about the stigma and sins of Khoua Her. The Hangs also objected, and most said that though the family had resettled under the Hang clan name, they were really from the Kong clan. In the end, I thought, does it really matter? Six lives were gone, taken by their own mother. What desperation had driven her? The Hmong clan system hadn't worked to protect the children.

The pain eventually became unbearable. My mom and sister were in the delivery room with me. They were noisy. At 4 AM, after twenty hours of labor, my animist and ritualistic mother, who had not been in a church for fifteen years, told my husband and sister to bow their heads in Christian prayer. My mother has a tendency to be melodramatic when stressed. She says now it was worse for her to watch me go through labor than to go through it herself five times. During labor, grief and love were both in my heart. I couldn't cry or scream. My life and Khoua Her's could have been exchanged but for a twist of fate. I had just ended up in a better place.

What could have driven Khoua Her to murder her own children? Growing up with two parents who took turns being depressed, angry, and, yes, hopeless, I had kept myself resilient and strong. If I had slammed the door of optimism and given up on myself, my younger siblings would have been without an emotional anchor. My positive attitude kept them going. I could tell that when I was dark and angry it made the three of them that way, too. As the second of five children, I felt it was my job to take care of the younger ones. Once, in middle school, I had come close to seeing death for myself as a solution. I turned myself around by realizing that other people's low expectations and opinions of me should not shape my future. Somehow, I pulled myself out of depression. My older sister had married after her freshman year at Mankato State University. Untethered, my life was empty and lonely in my early twenties without her. The helplessness and despair of my adolescence had been hard. Even so, I had endured. Also, I couldn't imagine either of my parents feeling as desperate as Khoua Her did.

The doctor used forceps to pull our son out. I was exhausted and couldn't push anymore. The baby's heartbeat was failing, and the doctor placed an IV to keep my contractions going. I had squeezed Lu's hand so hard and for so many hours that there were red welts around his ring finger. Once the baby was out, the doctor placed him onto my chest. Lu cut the baby's umbilical cord. I looked down and saw his perfect dark red lips, tiny wrinkled face, and helmet of black hair. His hair had grown past his ears. He was the most beautiful creature I had ever seen. My eyes welled up with tears, and after twenty hours of no screaming, hollering, or making noises, I started crying with relief, joy, and sadness. Khoua had delivered six babies like this, given life like this six times, and taken life six times. I whispered my son's name for the first time, *Fuchi*, and kissed his head. For someone who hadn't wanted motherhood, motherhood suited me perfectly. I would go on to have another three exceptionally perfect babies.

While I recuperated at Regions Hospital with Fuchi, I learned more about Khoua Her. She would stand trial and be jailed for life. She had failed at committing suicide. Back at work, I helped the community heal from the aftermath at McDonough Homes. I learned more about Khoua's life. She was married off at the age of twelve in a Thai refugee camp. She had given birth to a baby every year with no reprieve. In Thailand, if you were a young person who wanted to resettle in the United States and your parents refused to resettle, you were stuck in the refugee camps until you turned eighteen. The only way to overcome this hurdle was to marry and file to resettle as your own household. This policy created many teen marriages. When tragedy and trauma was all around, Hmong daughters who were orphans were bartered off like chattel to other clans in the refugee camps. I don't know if either scenario was true in Khoua's case, but since I had worked in Ban Napho refugee camp, I knew firsthand the rules of resettlement. The Hmong community is not kind to orphans, widows, and divorcées. Khoua was socially isolated. She was a battered woman. Her husband had abandoned her and the children. There had been seventeen police calls for service to her public housing unit. The public housing agency and the community policing program had responded, but there were no documented attempts to support the family's needs. Their battered and shattered lives, sadly, had been an "open secret" to the system with little formal action. Help had been within reach, yet also so far away.

There were no mental health services in St. Paul that could have been offered to her in a culturally and linguistically relevant way in 1996. We had perhaps one fully licensed Hmong mental health professional to serve the entire Hmong community in Minnesota. There were no women's shelters with advocates who could speak the Hmong language to help protect her and her children. What would become Asian Women United, the first battered women's shelter for Asian women in Minnesota, had just started after a group of young women had successfully advocated for resources from the state. When Jon Gutzmann, the executive director of the St. Paul Public Housing Agency, called a meeting to discuss how he could help, only two Hmong community members showed up. I was one of them. Unfortunately, I couldn't contain my anger and resentment. In a rare fit of temper, I told him how I felt about the situation and what his organization could have done earlier. Instead of being angry or offended, Jon eventually hired me to help fix the system as the Resident Services director. We planted a tree for each child who had died, including plaques with their names, outside of the McDonough Homes Community Center. Every time I go there, I still visit.

One of my first projects as the Resident Services director was to devise a protocol with the St. Paul Police to send social workers to public housing units after three calls for service and to offer family supports. Neither the Hmong cultural systems nor the public systems had worked for Khoua and her children. I have spent my life and career working to prevent such tragedies from happening ever again. This case was so traumatic, it followed me to my next job as the director of Adult Services in Ramsey

County. The State of Minnesota did an extensive mortality review, and I was interviewed to see where state systems might have failed in both adult's and children's services. This case followed me back to Wilder as the director of Children and Family Services, where I worked to create a clinical training institute to get more clinicians of color fully licensed and credentialed as mental health professionals. The case followed me to my role as president and CEO of the Wilder Foundation. In September 2018, I talked to the *Pioneer Press* about this case once more. I gave an overview of the expansion of mental health services to the Hmong community and new refugee and immigrant communities, and how this has changed in twenty years. It's still not happening quickly enough.

My son, Fuchi, turned twenty on September 5, 2018. His birthday also marks this tragedy. Twenty years later, it is broadly seen as the worst homicide case the city of St. Paul has ever experienced. Unfortunately, Khoua and her children are not unique. They represent the many families and people who are traded and dealt with like they are a cheap commodity because they are powerless and poor, left to suffer unprotected and ridiculed. They have few real choices to receive the support they need. Help comes too late, or it comes but with too many obligations and demands, creating more problems for those who are already suffering. Too often, instead of a hand up, we wait too long to give help and ask too much in return for those who are most in need. Birth and circumstance shouldn't determine destiny, but they often do.

Every year on Fuchi's birthday, I promise to use my privilege as a weapon for good. When I was younger and my world was restricted by what I could see and read, I felt invisible with few advantages. And yet, as I have seen families without stability or real opportunity, I understand the resilience and support I had, even in a family ravaged by war and trauma. I've chosen to believe that though I may be only one person, my passion and convictions, if applied diligently, can help save more families. Privilege is useless if we don't use it to benefit others. Over years of serving those most disadvantaged in society, I see that acts of love, support, and care have cost me nothing except having courage when moving forward is tough. When I am the only person of color, woman, class-crosser, or former refugee in a room, I willingly carry the voices of those who aren't visible in systems of power.

And now I know what my intense joy and sadness meant when I looked at Fuchi's face the first time. Women have divine right to give life. In Fuchi's innocent face, I saw a precious love unlike anything I had ever experienced before. I tell myself now that Khoua must have believed that suffering worse than death would come to her children if she was able to take her own life. She meant to kill herself. She just hadn't been successful. I won't ever know the truth, and now I don't want to know. I'd rather live with the fiction that it was both trauma and love that drove her to do what she did. But I do know this truth as the mother of four: when love is deliberately killed, all hope has expired. Some people tell me that hope can't keep people alive, but I believe it can, and it does. Some people tell me that hope can't be measured, but I believe it can because I have seen too many lives changed. Some people tell me that I can't see the bad in others because I am an eternal optimist; I tell them to leave me alone so I can do more good for humanity.

Dr. MayKao Y. Hang is vice president and inaugural dean of the College of Health at the University of St. Thomas and former president and CEO of the Amherst H. Wilder Foundation. She has dedicated her life to leading courageously, to improving lives today and for generations to come, and to social justice. Among her achievements, Dr. Hang is proud to be a current board member of the Minnesota Historical Society, a founding member and the inaugural board chair of the Coalition of Asian American Leaders (CAAL), and a cofounder of Hnub Tshiab: Hmong Women Achieving Together.

Orders

Duabhav BJ Lee

I'd say my family has a long history, a lineage, of service in the military, which fits oddly in the realm of the Hmong hierarchy of formalities, where one must address so-and-so based on relation to so-and-so. And thus, for a festive occasion this past summer, my cousin and her very general-like or type A husband were hosting a blessing dinner for my beloved uncle and aunt. All the tasks had been assigned, and my rather tall order was to enhance my meager pepper recipe to feed more than five hundred people. I laughed that day I was voluntold, saying, "I know my job, Brother! Don't worry. I got you."

Sure enough, the day of, the chaos of disorder erupted with my rather take-charge family colliding with the new church family that Uncle had embraced into his life. I was told to simply show up with my bags of peppers, and my ingredients would be present.

I watched the clock as I helped prepare other pieces of the day. Four hours before the dinner, I moved into the church's industrial kitchen. I put on a blue hairnet and gloves, then laid out my ingredients before me. Calmly, I informed my cousin we didn't have enough green onions. Frantically, she informed the designated person, and he called his number two, who was out buying other last-minute supplies. "They'll get some more. You do what you can until they get back," she said sternly.

The type A in me was flustered, but today wasn't about me; it was about honoring Uncle and Aunt and feeding the five-hundred-plus guests. I started dicing the red and green Thai peppers from my mother's garden on a large, white, circular cutting board. I refused to look at the clock when the supply of green onions appeared. One bushel. I shook my head and informed my cousin once again that it wasn't enough. She agreed. "I'll run to the store myself."

The photographer snapped a photo of me and said, "Use a blender." I rolled my eyes and replied, "I always hand cut everything when I make my pepper."

Slowly, I prepared the cilantro. Still no cousin. I washed the limes and began to cut them into slices. Still no cousin. I diced a third bag of peppers. Still no cousin. As I changed knives yet again, she came running in with the green onions. We stood silent in agreement like soldiers on a battlefield signaling codes that only Hmong women would know and recognize in the heat of battle. I quickly rinsed the onions she had brought, which were fresher than the previous bushel I had been given, and quickly diced them.

Peppers, cilantro, green onions, limes, two bottles of water, two bottles of fish sauce, and finally salt.

A church member helping with the cooking stopped and watched me. "You must make good pepper sauce if you were asked to make it for the dinner." I laughed nervously as I put the finishing touches into the sauce, as I had done for countless family gatherings before.

"How is it?" she inquired.

"I don't know."

"Let me go get some meat, and we'll try it together."

As I stirred the concoction, the girl reappeared with three thinly sliced pieces of roasted beef. We each took a slice and dipped it into a small portion of the pepper sauce. I looked to her for reaction first.

"It's good." She smiled. We both laughed, and I put the large bowl of pepper sauce into the refrigerator. It needed to sit before being added to the buffet line.

In all the commotion of the day, I wasn't able to grab a bit of that pepper sauce with my own plate that night.

Months later, my cousin's general-of-a-husband sat down next to me and said that my pepper was very popular.

I replied, "Brother, I wasn't asked to make my pepper. It was an order."

He laughed.

Duabhav BJ Lee is a born and raised Hmong southern belle trying to write about what moves her, shakes her, and makes her laugh.

Braving Imperfections

Douachee Vang

They always praised how smart I was, saying I could accomplish anything and everything if I just worked hard enough. But they also rebuked me by saying that only rich people could afford to dream and get what they want.

They always applauded how hardworking I was, telling others it would be impossible to host big parties without my help. But they also condemned me for being lazy when I put my studies first.

They always mentioned how much they loved me and how proud they were of everything I accomplished. But they also ridiculed me for choosing my career path and punished me even when they knew I was in pain.

This is what I've learned: people can be there to either hurt you or help you, and sometimes, they do both without even knowing it. That's why it makes me wonder: when can I find fault with the hurt that they give me, and when is it okay to accept the hurt as helping me?

I was conflicted.

No.

I still am.

They came from a land of war and little opportunities to a land that offers the "American Dream." With a handful of hope they pushed us children to achieve only greatness. I didn't see anything wrong with that. I wanted to succeed for them; I wanted to make them proud; I wanted to show them that anything is possible, just as they had told me. I wanted to be the leader they always dreamt of for each of us kids.

However, when does it become too much? When does the encouragement and the pushing become excessive, a detriment? When is the tough love unbearable to the point of toxicity?

Is it when I come home after 9 PM , from attending zero period in the morning to a four-hour after-school practice, to a mess in the kitchen? Since I was not present to do my gender role duties, I am punished with late-night chores out of spite. Or is it when they continually complain that I should have been like my friend or cousin who made the "right choices" by sticking to academics and quitting extracurricular activities? Or is it when I stay in the college library to study all night and get accused of being a "poj laib"?

I couldn't understand. I do everything that is asked of me and sometimes more. I held back on having a social life because I was lectured that "schoolwork can be done at home." I am told to be different from everyone else, yet I am also criticized for not being like everyone else. At family meetings I am told to "ua siab ntev" with my parents and just do what I am told because, as a Hmong woman, I have no agency or power.

I was tormented.

Distraught.

Depressed.

I went into seclusion at the age of twelve. It was then that Depression opened its arms to me, cradling my battered sense of self with such tenderness by giving me the attention and care I was yearning for. It let me weep and vent; it let me dream and scream. It was there to hold my hand when I etched rays of warm crimson tears onto my soft, thin skin. I *wanted* to feel pain, any kind of pain that could take away all of the hurt I was feeling at home. I thought if I could find another outlet of discomfort it would numb the hurt that my family was causing me. Yet I didn't feel anything. I couldn't. The pain I was searching for as a replacement was shrouded already by my sore heart and burning throat, by the confusion of what my identity really was or could be, and the questioning of how to survive the path ahead of me, while at the same time desiring to end it all.

Too often I asked myself: Should I be the sedentary filial Hmong daughter they desire of me? If so, that meant suppressing my ambitions and my determination. It meant limiting my fiery spirit and taming my inquisitive soul. Or should I be the outspoken and stubbornly radical Hmong daughter who they believe will suffer in the future if I don't live life the way they want me to? If so, that meant creating tension and tears at home. At a loss, I searched for answers.

When I opened up to others, they told me to ease up, to be more lenient with my parents, to remember the turmoil they went through in the Secret War. However, people didn't seem to understand the emotional roller coaster I have been on and that I am still on. It is challenging to be understood, knowing our parents' and grandparents' history of escaping war and genocide to give us children a safer and better future—something I will always be grateful for.

Nevertheless, I want to say that it is okay to not have that emotional, parental support. As long as you hold on to what is important to you and are determined to face the obstacles that will come your way, you can succeed. Because—let's be real—you won't truly know what you're getting yourself into until you're in the middle of it. As a result, I wish for the past to not be used as a weapon to police the present and the future, especially in emotionally abusive ways, such as my experience.

I am sure people may retort that I am too uncompromising or "too young to understand." And while these accusations may hold true to an extent, it does not make me selfish or unaccountable. I am simply speaking my truth.

I want people to know that they are not alone in having imperfections, in having mental illness, in having to deal with culture clash. I want people to know that even compromises and being understood may take time—often it can be longer than what we imagine or, frankly, it can be never. We have to face things that are uncomfortable sometimes because that is a part of surviving and thriving. Being able to face the uncomfortable things in my life has made me a leader and role model for myself, even though it wasn't easy, even though I am still learning.

Although it may be an anomaly to see oneself as one's own leader and role model, I view it as an empowering act. During my darkest days, I didn't have anyone I could safely and comfortably fall back to. I felt like an outcast sheep and as if I didn't belong anywhere. As I worked through the pain and gradually decided to make decisions for myself, my world grew bigger and I found the places where I could belong and the people whom I could look up to.

So this is to say, it *is* possible to be your own leader. You may not be able to recognize it now, but someday you will see how far you've come. If you surround yourself with people who understand and support you and you continue to believe in your passions, you can achieve anything. Most importantly, never forget your roots and your experiences because they are part of what makes you, *you.* As I am continually learning, being different is not so bad; it just takes some getting used to.

Looking back, I chose to do the things that made me who I am today. I chose to stay in concert, jazz, and marching band in high school; I chose to do clubs; I chose my women's studies major, anthropology minor, and Southeast Asian studies certificate in college. And now, I am choosing to do the things that will progressively let me grow. I am choosing to take a fifth year of undergraduate school, which will give me the opportunity to do research and gain all of the experiences I can get; I am choosing to apply for graduate school to be an academic scholar, something that is a new concept to my family; I am choosing to study out of state if that opportunity is given to me because I want to spread my wings as far as I can.

To close this narrative, I leave you with these words: As you navigate your way through life, don't be afraid to choose the path that is less traveled. As Ralph Waldo Emerson states, "Go instead where there is no path and leave a trail."

Lastly, where there is pain or discomfort, there is a story to be told. Don't be afraid to share it.

This is my story.

And it is still unfinished.

Douachee Vang majored in women's studies at Fresno State and was a Ronald E. McNair Scholar and a Michigan Humanities Emerging Research Scholar. She will complete her master's in cul-

tural studies at the University of Washington Bothell in spring 2020. Douachee is passionate about feminism, power and knowledge, and social media studies/activism. She hopes to contribute more/critical Hmong studies scholarship into academia and her community. In her free time, Douachee can be found watching YouTube or Netflix and, more importantly, writing her feelings out. Her written work has appeared in zines and small anthologies. She is actively learning and unlearning, dismantling, and surviving.

Profile of a Hmong Leader

Kao Kalia Yang

Dawb had long, thick hair. She walked slowly. Somewhere in her earliest years, she had gotten very sick, lost consciousness. For weeks, she stopped talking entirely. Her snot was green and thick. It took her long months to learn how to speak again. Some people called her stupid. Others said that she was handicapped. Lots of people said, "If Dawb can do it, so can you, you, and you."

Dawb was a year and nine months older than me. She was my only sibling for the first eight years of my life. I adored her.

In Thailand, crossing a bridge of flooded rocks in a rainstorm, I lost one of my flip-flops to the rushing currents. It was Dawb who jumped into the sewage canal, as my older cousins and I watched, to retrieve the errant shoe for me, dirty water flooding into her mouth, covering her head.

In America, it was Dawb who looked up at the bully girl towering over us on the school bus and demanding, "Which of you opened this window when I said no one could?" I had opened the window, but I shook in my seat as Dawb raised her hand and then closed her eyes. I watched as the big girl's fisted hand fell hard over my sister's head. There was a dull thud and then silence as the mean girl walked away.

All of our life together, Dawb has given me many reasons to see her courage, her sacrifice, her love.

When Dawb won the North End Elementary School spelling bee a year and a half after our arrival in America, I knew that school was going to be easy for her and that she was going to give our parents' dreams room to grow here.

Dawb was the first girl in our family to successfully graduate with her bachelor of arts degree.

When Dawb said she wanted to go to law school, an uncle who loved her said, "You're too short and small. No one would want to put their problems in your hands to help resolve. You should look into other jobs where someone of your stature won't be judged too harshly."

With the support of our mother and father, Dawb persisted and graduated from law school. She passed the bar and received her license to practice law in the state of Minnesota.

Dawb was the first person in our family to marry outside of the culture. She married a man from Kentucky, the first in his family to go to college, get a graduate education, and leave his community and home culture behind to discover a bigger world. They were well matched in many ways, but there was no way he could have attended to the rituals and traditions that governed a Hmong marriage, so they had a court ceremony and an abbreviated Hmong wedding picnic in our backyard.

Dawb was the first to have an interracial child, a little boy with light brown eyes, a thick head of coarse brown hair, and the most aquiline nose we'd ever seen in our family. Our mother named him Phoojywg, our language for friendship. Dawb was the first to have the second. She was raising a family, the likes of which we were discovering with each step she took.

In the mix of the marriage and the child rearing, Dawb became an experienced lawyer. She opened up an office at a Hmong market, put up a sign as "The Village Lawyer," and took in the paying clients and the nonpaying ones. She helped a distant uncle keep his home in a drawn-out case against nine big banks who had all, at different times, held the title to his modest house. Dawb represented a young Somali student sent to court in Morris, Minnesota, by two white students who felt that her presence was threatening to them because she'd said, "I can't even . . ." as they approached her in a full cafeteria. Dawb's done many things for many people, each time with an understanding in her heart that the earth is not even for everyone.

Late at night, her phone rings. Someone is in trouble and they need help. Early in the morning, her phone rings. Another person is concerned about someone else who may need help. Each time her phone rings, Dawb answers, her voice calm, "Hello, you've reached the Village Lawyer. How can I help you?"

Today, Dawb lives quietly with her family on the east side of

St. Paul. Her hair is not so thick as it once was, but she continues to walk slowly through the world, her head tilted high, listening for the call of the lonely birds. The little things don't bother her—she's had lots of experience dealing with them gracefully, the things people say about who or how she is, or how she will be judged. She focuses on the big things. She understands well that one day she will be judged by them.

Dawb Yaj does not mind when people say, "If Dawb can do it, so can you, you, and you."

Kao Kalia Yang is the author of The Latehomecomer: A Hmong Family Memoir, *winner of the 2009 Minnesota Book Award in creative nonfiction/memoir and readers' choice and a finalist for the PEN USA Award in creative nonfiction and the Asian Literary Award in nonfiction.* The Song Poet: A Memoir of My Father *won the 2016 Minnesota Book Award in creative nonfiction/ memoir and was a finalist for the National Book Critics Circle Award, the Chautauqua Prize, a PEN USA Award in nonfiction, and the Dayton's Literary Peace Prize. Her first children's book,* A Map Into the World, *debuted in 2019.*

Maum Tshis Coj Ntug: The Trailblazer

Kia M. Lor

Since childhood, I was known as the *maum tshis coj ntug* (the leader of the sheep herd) because I was born in the year of the sheep, in the sign of Aries. More than that, I was naturally a curious child who wandered around the city with my purple bike, leading my younger cousins and little sisters in what we called "journeys." Back in the day they called it *poj laib* (radical female rebel), when it was really *trailblazing*. I knew at a very young age that I was born a trailblazer, even though I didn't have the language for it then. I knew this because I deeply enjoyed exploring unknown territories and formulating new trails for people to follow.

However, growing up on government welfare in a single-parent household as a public-school-educated Hmong girl who would become the first person in her family to attend college made trailblazing an uphill challenge. No one in my family had ever ventured beyond the unknown territories of the Hmong circle. Consequently, the ethnocentric Hmong values ran deep in my community. Being female made it even harder to be a trailblazer because of the rigid cultural expectations. Gender roles for men and women were explicit: men were socialized to be bosses while women were socialized to be bossed, particularly to be a *nyab* (daughter-in-law). This rhetoric made me sick to my stomach. For all I know, I didn't qualify as a good *nyab* because of my mother's divorced reputation. People judged me based on her. "Like mother like daughter," they would say. Therefore, I didn't even stand a chance to be judged on my own merit as a *nyab*—not that I wanted to be a *nyab* anyway, because *nyab*s were forbidden to be trailblazers.

I had an unconventional mother who was always running in and out of marriages, battling her own addiction, and struggling with her own cultural limitations. At twelve years old, I suspected there was something fundamentally wrong with the fact that my mother was forced to marry and divorce her four abusive husbands because she couldn't opt out from the Hmong marriage game—a game in which she would remain the loser every time. She didn't speak English and she couldn't drive, which were two of the most essential skills to have in order to obtain autonomy.

I am the second child of six; more importantly, I was the first daughter. That meant I had the most responsibilities. Because of this, I found myself double cast as *a child* and *a parent*. At times I played the child who needed permission from my mother to do sleepovers, to add Hot Cheetos to the shopping cart, and to set up my own dentist appointments. Other times I played the parent who executed the payment of bills, translated at parent-teacher conferences for my siblings and me, and forged signatures on field trip permission slips. My unconventional mother was both a blessing and a curse. On one hand, I had to sacrifice my typical teenage experiences such as dating, clubbing, and shopping at name-brand stores; on the other hand, I learned how to be responsible and mature early on in life.

I didn't know this then, but in retrospect, this balancing act prepared me to be a cultural broker in the broader American political, cultural, and educational domains. Little did I know that my difficult and convoluted years of firsthand experience growing up on government welfare in a single-parent household as a public-schooled, first-generation, Hmong, female college student would grant me first-class access to a wealth of empathy, tenacity, and bravery.

I remember how my mother used to compare herself with the knife and me with the pencil. She said, "I can control the knife gracefully. I would never die from starvation because of my mastery in cooking." On the other hand, I was very skilled with the pencil, something she wasn't. She said my ability to control the pencil would grant our stories eternal life. Therefore reading, writing, and literacy became my tools of emancipation.

To me, education had always been my escape route away from all the cultural and financial problems at home, and quite frankly I excelled in the classroom. At school I was judged on my own merit, on my ability to produce knowledge, to reiterate concepts and theories, and to intentionally reflect on my own experiences. In the classroom I was praised for my eloquence, my intellectual contributions, and my critical opinions. On top of that, I was encouraged to be a leader in the National Honor Society, Link Crew, and various other clubs and organizations. I was encouraged to be a trailblazer. If trailblazing was my fire, education kindled it. Through my achievements in education I began rejecting Hmong patriarchal values because I found them oppressive and unfair.

College wasn't in my scheme until junior year of high school, which was pretty late. I owe a great deal of my educational success to many mentors, guidance counselors, and organizations such as the Hmong Women's Circle, Youth Leadership Initiative, HmoobTeen, and the First Step Program, who believed in me and gave me instruments to access higher education. I scored a one-way ticket out of poverty the moment I received the Gates Millennium Scholarship. For me it was the golden ticket to any college or university in the United States. It was as if my entire life had prepared me for this scholarship—the overbearing poverty, the unstable single parent, the struggle of being a political refugee, and the unending cycle of sexist oppression. Going to college was my intervention to end the cycle of oppression in my family. *Or so I thought.*

Little did I know I was exiting one system of oppression only to enter another. I faced tremendous contradictions in my educational career. At an institutional level, I found it disheartening that educational access and success in college for traditionally underrepresented populations remained a serious problem, most notably students from low-income, first-generation, non-native-English-speaking, and specific racial/ethnic groups. At a personal level, I found myself conflicted about my bicultural identity, struggling to reconcile my *Hmong* and *American* identities. I remember continuously fighting for my right to be treated fairly as an American student who was from the Twin Cities (not from abroad), who spoke English fluently, and who was just as deserving and smart as all the other, mostly white students.

Being a Hmong person in a predominately white institution

such as the College of St. Benedict in central Minnesota, my experience of "college" was drastically different from that of my white friends. Most Hmong students didn't study abroad because most of them could not afford to. I was only able to do it because I had a full-ride scholarship. In fact, the concept of studying abroad is so bizarre that when I introduced my mother to the fact that I would spend five months each in India and China, she was shocked as to why I would want to study in a developing country. "The US has the best education system in the world, and most students around the world would die to be in your shoes!" she exclaimed. She reminded me of how she survived the Vietnam War just to bring me to the United States so I could receive the best education in the world. She wanted me to be educated as an American. I told her that studying abroad was what educated Americans do.

While abroad, I observed the ubiquitous tensions in racial and ethnic relations between white American students and American students of color (I was the only Asian girl in both programs). I was astonished to see how white privilege manifested during my semesters abroad, and taken aback as to how unfairly I was treated compared to my white colleagues. Frustrated with the discrimination, I returned to campus and tearfully expressed my concerns to many professors and study abroad directors. Though they offered sympathy, they were ill prepared to give me the comfort and validation I needed. From that point on I concluded that higher education institutions needed to reconsider prior beliefs about and strategies for educating a different population of students, especially minority students like me.

There is no doubt my scholarship and my desire to attain higher education has put me on a trajectory beyond my childhood circumstances. It has indeed afforded me the social and financial mobility to explore uncharted territories that my family would never be able to provide me, territories such as my two study abroad experiences in both India and China and privileged spaces such as the College of St. Benedict and the University of Pennsylvania. I am enormously grateful.

However, it would be dishonest of me to not address the social reproductive system of education, a system that trains the wealthy to take up places at the top of the economy and conditions the poor to accept lowly status in class structure. It would be disingenuous of me to not recognize the problematic neoliberal discourse used by higher education institutions to recruit low-income, high-achieving students like me. Individualism, college as success, social upward mobility, and the "yes you can" rhetoric are some of the major components of the neoliberal discourse used by recruiters. Higher education has provided a safe, comfortable, and secure space *away* from poverty, but has it taken me *out* of poverty? Can I really use the master's tools to dismantle the master's house? That I am still trying to figure out.

What I know for sure is this: Education has given me critical skills to differentiate what is truth and what is perspective. Education has acted as a microphone to amplify my voice. Education has transformed my understanding of social justice. As a trailblazer who is, among other things, a high-achieving Hmong woman, refugee, and first-generation college student, I believe it has always been in me to contribute to the development of international education, multicultural education, and diversity in education. I was born to formulate new trails for people to follow. I believe it is education's responsibility to be a space of reflection, transformation, and liberation.

Kia M. Lor was born in a Thai refugee camp and came to the United States with her family when she was four years old. She is the second of six children and the eldest daughter. At a young age, Kia acquired skills to be a cultural broker between her immigrant mother and the mainstream American culture. Today, she acts as an academic cultural broker as assistant director of Language and Intercultural Learning at the Fries Center for Global Studies at Wesleyan University in Middletown, Connecticut. Kia is also an active fellow at the Intercultural Communication Institute in Portland, Oregon.

Craving to Be a Hmong Woman

Npaus Baim Her

It was near the end of my elementary school years when we all sat around the table and the white English as a second language teacher asked a simple question about our favorite colors. Being last to answer, I thought about my favorite color while Chue, Vang, and Lee each took turns to answer the question. At the time, I liked yellow, but it seemed too plain of an answer, so I said white. In my mind, I imagined a white wall. It was a color so easily painted over, transforming to any color I desired. I enjoyed the thought: liking every color.

I was so excited to give my answer and the reason behind it. I thought it was the coolest answer of all. When I said my favorite color was white, Chue said, "That's because you like white people." I can clearly remember the words slipping out of his lips and the way he looked at me with a smile on his face showing his big teeth. His eyelids squeezed together almost as if they were closed because of his cheeks. My mouth dropped, and I denied it immediately, saying, "No!" After that, everything's a blur. I do not remember if the teacher said anything. I do not remember if Chue replied back to me. I do not remember if I told him my reason or if the words "I do not like white people" slipped out of my lips.

Chue had always used words against me to keep a distance between us. Lee was being influenced by his actions and started to also tease me. Vang did not tease me, but he would not stick up for me, either. Those words made me feel as if I was just some Hmong girl who could not speak her cultural language and was whitewashed for hanging out with only white people.

I spent the rest of my elementary school time trying to prove to Chue that I am truly Hmong. I felt the need to have him accept me for being Hmong, but really, all I wanted was to find a place to belong. However, I couldn't do that with three Hmong boys.

Middle school was starting, and I was filled with excitement. Different elementary schools from the district came together to attend one middle school, meaning I was finally not going to be the only Hmong girl in a whole grade. Unfortunately, in the first two years of middle school, things were not going well with making new Hmong friends who were girls. The girls I met were a year older, and in middle school, that age gap feels huge. I tried so hard to fit in with them, but ended up becoming an annoying person instead. I knew it, too. I became someone I was not proud of. Not only that, I was not developing a sense of Hmong identity with them as I had hoped. I thought if I could find Hmong friends, I would finally be Hmong. In the end, I could still hear Chue calling me "whitewashed."

During this identity crisis, a few Hmong girls and I were invited to join a Hmong Girl's Reading Circle created by a Hmong staff member, Malia Yang-Xiong. Together, we read the first Hmong book I was ever exposed to: *Hey, Hmong Girl, Whassup?: The Journal of Choua Vang* by Leah Rempel (2004). It was a fictional story about a girl who wrote about her experiences and expectations of being a traditional Hmong daughter. This story discusses the traditional gender roles placed on Hmong girls during the early migration to the United States, roles that restrict them from pursuing an education and career path. Some common issues were teen pregnancy, early marriage, and commitment to younger siblings as well as household chores.

I was addicted to *Hey, Hmong Girl, Whassup?* and constantly read ahead of everyone. I couldn't help but continue to turn each page! I wanted to know about other Hmong experiences, and unexpectedly, I was craving to explore my Hmong woman identity. In the reading circle, Mrs. Xiong encouraged us to read up to certain pages, so when we come back as a group, we could reflect on our own Hmong woman identity. She told us this situation may have happened to many Hmong women and maybe it was happening in our lives. Whenever she discussed or questioned the circle, I could see the excitement in her face waiting for us to answer as she made eye contact with each and every one of the girls. Her excitement to hear our answers encouraged me to engage with her.

Mrs. Xiong and I developed a close relationship, and I fail to remember the chronological order of our experiences together. However, I will never forget the memories made. Maybe sometime during or after the Hmong Girl's Reading Circle, Mrs. Xiong invited me to explore the Minnesota History Museum with her. She probably saw my eagerness to understand my Hmong woman identity and was trying to help satisfy my craving. There, shows and stands were sharing Asian cultures and traditions. It was my first time at the Minnesota History Museum. As we entered the building and walked up the staircase, we first encountered a set of tools displayed behind a glass case. The tools looked like small versions of a pickax. A Hmong woman asked those around if we had ever seen this tool and to guess what it could be used for. After I and others placed a guess, she revealed that the tool made ripples in Hmong skirts. It blew my mind because never had I questioned what made ripples in Hmong skirts. I realized I had never questioned many Hmong cultural aspects when I should have been curious by exposing myself to such rich traditions.

When the last year of middle school came, I was more confident to accept my identity without someone else's approval. Chue's words were no longer echoing in my ears. It was thanks to Mrs. Xiong's guidance and because I was learning to be myself. I was finally making friends with people I could connect with. After the Hmong Girl's Reading Circle, I no longer met with Mrs. Xiong and had to explore how to expose myself to empowerment and different experiences. I saw flyers about after-school clubs and joined Culture Club and Journey. Coincidentally, Mrs. Xiong and I crossed paths again because she was involved in both clubs. In Culture Club, she made the students think critically about how to express ourselves through activities, such as writing poetry. I learned about different ethnicities and their cultures. In

Journey, we did activities to build our leadership skills, and she would always tell me how she could see a leader within me.

Now I am a first-year graduate student. I have learned not only to expose myself to a variety of new experiences but also to involve myself in the community. I've developed a passion to create visual designs of my Hmong woman identity because I'm still learning to understand that identity. I also collect stories of Hmong elders because I'm still curious about Hmong history and culture. What I'm doing isn't only to satisfy my cravings; it's also to give something back to the community, especially the youth. Mrs. Xiong's guidance and empowerment made me reflect on my Hmong woman identity and taught me to always ask questions if I'm curious. I express my thanks to her by inviting her to my small art exhibits. Each time she attends, she has the same excitement I saw back in middle school during the Hmong Girl's Reading Circle. She looks at my art and smiles throughout the whole showing. After, she comes to talk to me, saying, "I always knew you had a leader within you."

Npaus Baim Her is furthering her education through University of Minnesota Duluth's English master's program and has been given the opportunity to teach college writing as a graduate instructor. She serves as secretary on the board of directors for a nonprofit organization, Minors, and also volunteers as a writing assistant, collecting Secret War stories for the organization's book project to educate Hmong youth about their elders' history. She has exhibited her art and literary work with HECUA (Higher Education Consortium for Urban Affairs) Alumni, Prior Affairs, and the Coalition of Asian American Leaders.

Breaking Worlds

Renee Ya

I was fifteen years old, and it was a hot day in May. In Fresno, summer starts early, and beads of sweat were building behind my knees and on my neck. The sun was beating down on me as I walked to the mailbox to retrieve the mail. I was anxiously waiting for my test results. I remember seeing the envelope addressed to me: Renee Ya. The "From" address said "California High School Proficiency Exam," also known as the CHSPE: passing this exam allows you to receive a certificate of proficiency in high school, which translates to the equivalent of receiving a high school diploma so you can continue on to higher education such as vocational schooling, community college, or a university. And as I ran my fingers across the lettering of the envelope, a jolt of energy carried me swiftly past five houses and back through my front door.

"Daddy! Daddy! It's finally here! My test results are back!" He knew exactly what I was talking about. I had taken the exam about six weeks prior, and every day that passed left my stomach in a knot.

"Well, open it!" He sat up from the couch excitedly.

"I . . . can't! I'm too nervous." I pushed the unopened envelope to him.

He grabbed the edge and ripped it down the side, careful to not tear the paper within. He upended it into his hand and opened the letter. He screamed.

"AYYIA!!! YOU PASSED!" He grabbed me in his arms, and we jumped up and down.

"I passed? I PASSED!"

A simple letter stating that I had successfully completed the CHSPE meant that I was on my way to college.

I chose DeVry University in Fremont, California, because it allowed me to get an accredited undergrad degree within two years. The university also had a lot of Hmong students due to its accelerated engineering programs, and it had an established Hmong student club.

I had already started attending community college classes while at Sunnyside High School in Fresno, so even though I was the youngest student, I walked in having completed four of the required general education classes.

Going to college, I was relentless. I continued to take community college courses both online as well as in person during the weekends and during summer and winter breaks. I had petitioned DeVry to allow me to pile on as many classes as I could take based on the prerequisites I had, sometimes as many as thirty-two credit units (or the equivalent of nine classes) in a semester. They begrudgingly allowed it, cautioning that I needed to maintain a certain GPA; otherwise, my privilege of taking so many classes would be revoked.

I made sure I passed all of my classes.

I took out student loans. I applied for scholarships and grants. My parents had dropped everything in Fresno to move to Fremont so that I could go to school without worrying about paying rent, but I used much of my student loans to help.

I took on part-time jobs, one working on campus as an administrative assistant in the registrar's office; others were paid internships.

For two semesters I also was president of the Hmong Club, its first Hmong woman president. I made the club inclusive, and the intersection of Asian, White, Black, and Latino students in the club made it the most diverse organization on campus. We fundraised, held movie and game nights, and even had an honorary senior banquet to send off the graduating class of Hmong students, whether they were active members or not.

One of my fondest memories was having White, Black, and Hmong students perform a traditional Hmong dance out of appreciation of the Hmong culture. This included ensuring that the performers got suits custom made and tailored for taller, bigger bodies since they weren't able to just borrow something from a cousin of mine.

It wasn't the first time I fought for inclusion within stuffy rooms full of much older men who believed in the "good ol' days," surrounding themselves with a "boys club" of friends and family to prove their point—and it wouldn't be the last time. Each time felt like a different world with different rules, all very difficult to navigate, all long uncontested.

Despite harsh criticism from distantly related uncles that I was a "poj laib" (bad girl) for my wildly colored hair and Americanized attitude toward assimilating and accepting assistance from non-Hmong people, I defied their crass comments and let them roll off me like water on feathers. I stayed focused on my goals.

I graduated from DeVry University within six trimesters, which is exactly two years, and walked across the stage to receive my bachelor of science in business administration at the age of seventeen in 2004: the youngest in the school's entire seventy-plus-year history and the youngest in the Hmong society as I knew it.

But I didn't want the pomp and circumstance. I just wanted to keep driving forward.

I had a few choices as to what to do next. I could either pursue a master's degree or go straight into the workforce. I decided that I wanted to do both. I had gotten accepted to begin my master's in information systems management from DeVry's Keller Graduate School of Management and also accepted a job in the video game industry as a quality assurance tester and game designer. I had to wait more than a month before I could start working because I had to be eighteen to put in the number of hours expected in the industry.

I thought it would be a regular forty-hour workweek. I ended up working more than eighty hours a week for the six months I was there, in addition to taking four classes for my graduate school.

While the student loans and working part-time had helped to cover some living expenses, once I started working full-time I was finally able to offer my family a more comfortable life, as almost my entire paychecks went to paying rent, utilities, and food. I wanted to give back to the people who believed in me most—my family.

In my first three years in the video game industry, I jumped around to about six different companies, staying for between three to seven months. Because each studio goes through game development cycles, hopping from one company to another, only to return to the previous company the next year, was par for the course and what it takes to make it in the industry. But this instability made for a sour taste in my family's mouth. Why couldn't I stay at one company for fifteen years like my parents had? Was I so irresponsible?

Eventually the stress was too much, and my parents moved back to Fresno. By then I was living alone in San Francisco—The City! It was my dream. But sadness clouded my excitement, as single life reflected poorly on my family. I was a disobedient daughter for leaving home before getting married.

Another issue arose: I was also very young. Though I was now two years into my career, having put in the eighty-plus-hour weeks, showing my expertise at adaptability and understanding company needs, surely my request to be considered for an assistant lead role in an attempt at upward mobility wouldn't fall on deaf ears. Yes, I was nineteen-almost-twenty by this point, but I had an undergraduate degree, was working on a master's, and knew I showed promise that I could take on more responsibility. My boss shrugged me off. "Oh, you're way too young for anyone to take you seriously. Can you imagine someone twice your age wanted to listen to you?"

That comment stung. It pierced my heart and wrenched tears from my eyes. Seeing this, my boss abruptly left—"Uh, I have another meeting I have to attend"—and left me in the conference room, sobbing.

I went to the human resources department to decry ageism. I had written up the incident, timestamped and expertly noted each word and reaction. I wanted to let the company know that I wouldn't allow this setback to stop me from moving forward with my career goals. And where I thought I would be met with hesitation and dismissiveness, I was met with warmth and genuine concern.

My boss was reprimanded. The HR team who handled my case told me that my boss was sent for sensitivity training; they followed up with me to ensure that my boss didn't retaliate against me. I felt that this group of women knew what discrimination in the workforce looked like. But the damage had already been done.

When I applied for an assistant lead position, my request for transfer was denied. I soon put in my two-week letter of resignation. As I was walking out the door, the division's vice president pulled me aside for a quick coffee chat. She wanted to let me know that if I changed my mind, she would hire me for an administrative role under her. I thanked her and declined. My heart was in game development work.

I finally had my big break: the next company I went to was a video game start-up working on massively multiplayer online games, or MMOs. I had bosses who championed my growth. They took me under their wing and mentored me. I was able to go from lead quality assurance tester to project coordinator under marketing and public relations. I ran marketing communications, gave demos of the game, produced media assets, hosted press events. I was finally being recognized for the work I was capable of doing because I had people who believed in me.

And yet, I was plagued by another glaring issue. The industry was male dominated, and I was a (1) young, (2) female, (3) Asian minority. What some would call "A Triple Threat." I had no place telling people much older than me what to do. Certainly a woman couldn't understand the complexity of the technology that was being created to run the game. Was I even from the United States? I wouldn't be able to understand our older, male, American target audience.

I was baffled.

I would sit in incredibly important strategic meetings and male engineers would look right through me as if I wasn't even there. Or I was relegated to being the notetaker, fetching water and drinks from the break room, making photocopies or printouts of the design documents we were reviewing. The oppression of the industry towered over me, loomed over me, ready to topple my existence and suffocate me.

And then the company went bankrupt. This happened often. Or the company was purchased and everyone was let go.

Then you would have to reset at a totally new company. Maybe you'd see familiar faces of those you'd worked with from ghost game studios that disappeared like the vaporware technology they were trying to create. But it always happened the same way.

They would start with the first few rounds of layoffs. A mandatory "all-hands" meeting for half of the company. The other half was in a different mandatory all-hands meeting. Of course, the first half were the ones who were let go, usually with no severance. Maybe you could get your accrued vacation paid out to you. The second all-hands meeting would be reassurance that they were just trimming the fat and that this was the team they were going to move forward with. Except they miscalculated, and then they had to do a second round of layoffs. The setup was the same: two separate mandatory all hands for two different groups. And this process would continue until it was just the last few standing as the assets were liquidated, and the few remaining IT members would scrub hard drives of intellectual property before sending the hardware to consignment shops.

Discarded humans, discarded technology.

I became very good at recognizing this pattern and thought I would be able to avoid this scenario playing out for the people in my department.

By the time I was twenty-five, I was employed by a very well-off Chinese MMO company based out of Beijing. They had a US and a European office so they could expand their market reach. I had managed to work my way into running a department of fifteen individuals: a product manager, three project managers, five quality assurance testers, two front-end web developers, and five designers. We ran the gamut when it came to publishing the games and their various updates in the United States and Europe. We were visionaries when it came to the future of the company.

I remember distinctly when an executive from the Beijing office came to the United States to interview each team and explore how they worked with other Beijing counterparts. I was called out in a meeting that included both my peers and my boss: "Why should we have you in this position when you are duplicating work of someone in Beijing?"

For every question, I had a good, poignant answer. I was articulate. I was calm and decisive. And my boss was completely silent.

I knew he needed me to defend myself because had he shown

any sort of loyalty to me, this executive could say that my boss was not someone who could make good hiring decisions and remove him from the equation. But if I was defending myself to an older, Asian male executive, the most they could do was fire me. My boss thought only of himself in that moment, and I felt betrayal for all the thankless work I did for the company.

Yet again, management made bad decisions, which ended up in the same pattern, and my entire team was ripped out from under me; I had no say in the matter. Behind closed doors, executives made decisions based on an arbitrary percentage generated by performance and individual employee contribution to the company with no feedback from anyone.

I put in my two-weeks' notice. I couldn't believe the cascading layoffs had happened again, this time under my watch—or so I thought. I beat myself up over the decision, lamenting how I could have tried harder, could have managed upward to my boss and other executives to have a bigger influence. But then I thought, "Why should I feel so guilty about something over which I really had no control?"

Finally, at the age of twenty-eight, I figured that with more than ten years of experience working from entry to running a global division, I could open up my own technology and media company. I named it Tiger Byte Studios, an homage to the Hmong word *tsov tom* (tigerbite)—reclaiming a curse uttered to us by parents.

Tsov tom is used as a way to bring us down, to denote how we are unintelligent. Only an unintelligent person would approach a tiger and get bit. While tigers are seen in the Hmong culture as dangerous deities, transforming into human forms to lure us away and to infiltrate our huts and family members, it makes sense that *tsov tom* can be culturally one of the worst things to say to someone.

However, tigers are also seen as powerful and majestic beasts who are protected and highly guarded as special endangered species.

I wanted to use the words as empowerment.

I currently employ a product manager, two software developers, a project manager, three 3-D artists, one 2-D artist, and two quality assurance testers.

We launched one game within the first year of founding the company, created a back-end platform that connects to our player base in real time, are currently working on other mobile video games, and offer other services to the Hmong community such as outreach and education.

Had it not been for more than thirteen years of continuous grinding, I know that I wouldn't have been as experienced a business owner and leader in the industry as I am now. Without my trials of dealing with ageism, sexism, and poor management decisions, I could not begin to comprehend how to be a good mentor and leader.

Through my career I have tried to foster inclusion and diversity, because in the end, we should all strive to leave someone with more than when we found them. We need to be the change we want to see. For me, that meant seeking out other women from the industry via LinkedIn, industry meetups, and attending conferences.

If you had told fifteen-year-old Renee that she would grow to become the type of person who received inquiries from prospective mentees, requests to be a special guest speaker at conference plenary panels, or proposals to lead workshops on video game career development, she probably would have been speechless and humbled to think that such opportunities could be available. With each opportunity, I remind myself that the sweat from the hard work of breaking worlds will help to create the path for others to follow.

Renee Ya grew up in Fresno, California. An accomplished creative type, she has published photography pieces in the Smithsonian's "On This Day" web series, contributed poetry and prose to several web magazines, and is the secretary of the Science Fiction Poetry Association. She spends her days vanquishing evil spirits in the name of the moon in the San Francisco Bay Area. When she's not saving the world, she's a product manager in the video game industry by trade and mother to the next feisty generation of women warriors. Learn more at reneeya.com or follow her on Twitter @dnldreams.

Impossible Dream

Gaosong V. Heu

In the spring of 2017, Gaosong Vang Heu's parents decided it was time to throw Gaosong a graduation party. Despite being two years out of school, Gaosong spent several nights tossing and turning, spending every minute up until the party trying to capture her journey as a Hmong American woman in higher education and in the arts. Gaosong V. Heu gave a speech and performance on June 24, 2017, at White Dragon Hall in Maplewood, Minnesota, in celebration of the college graduations of her and her brother, Dr. Fue Vang.

Ntawm no, kuv lub npe hus uas Nkauj Ntxhoo Vaj Hawj.
(My name is Gaosong Vang Heu.)

Ua ntej, kuv xav ua tsaug rau tag nrog kuv tsev neeg, cov tub ntxhais khiav dej num thiab ib tsoom phooj ywg sawv daws.
(Before I begin, I want to give thanks to everyone in my family, anyone who helped put this party together, and all of my friends.)

Yog tsis muaj nej tag nrog koom siab koom ntsws los txhawb peb lub rooj ua koob tsheej no, kuv thiab kuv tus nus yeej tsis muaj siab los hais lus raus saum lub sam thiaj hnub no.
(If you all did not come together as one to help support this celebration, my brother and I would not have the courage to come to this stage and speak today.)

Tshwj xeeb tshaj plaws, kuv xav hais ua tsaug rau kuv tus Txiv Mas Hawj, thiab kuv Niam Pog Txiv Yawg Txawj Liag Hawj.
(Most importantly, I want to say thank you to my husband, Marc Heu, and my father- and mother-in-law, Vincent and Elizabeth Heu.)

Nkawv tuaj tsis tau hnub no vim nkawv nyob rau French Guiana.
(They couldn't be here today because they live in French Guiana.)

Tiamsis, txawm neb nyob kev dev los, lub siab nyob ze.
(However, even though they are far, our hearts are near.)

Yog tsis muaj neb hlub thiab txhawb kuv txoj kev kawm ntawv, kuv yeej kawm ntawv tsis tau, thiab kuv yeej kawm tsis tiav.
(If I did not have your love and support in my educational career, I would not have been able to go to school and graduate.)

Neb xa nyiaj rau wb siv, neb coj kuv thiab Mas mus ua sis rau Fab Kis Teb los, kuv xav hais ua tsaug rau neb txoj kev hlub, thiab kev qhuab qhiab kom kuv thiab Mas mus ua neeg zoo.
(You both sent us money to live, you took Marc and myself to vacation in France. I want to say thank you for your love, and for the ways in which you both continue to teach and inspire us to be better human beings.)

Tsis tas lis ntawv, kuv xav hais ua tsaug rau kuv niam thiab kuv txiv Nom Yeeb Vaj thiab Paj Hawj Vaj.
(Moreover, I want to give thanks to my parents, Nao Ying Vang and Pang Her Vang.)

Txij thaum kuv yog ib tug mi nyuam ntxhais, neb yeej hlub thiab txhawb kuv lub zog.
(Ever since I was a little girl, you loved me and supported my efforts.)

Neb txoj kev hlub thiab tu kuv yug loj hlob, ua ib tug ntxhais muaj txuj ci, txawj ntse, thiab paub los hlub kuv tsev neeg thiab haiv neeg Hmoob.
(Your love and care have nurtured me to adulthood and allowed me to become a woman with talents, with smarts, who knows how to love my family and my Hmong people.)

Yeej tsis muaj lus coj los piav kom nqig siab kuv txoj kev hlub rau neb.
(There are no words to describe how much I love you both.)

Kuv thov kom kuv rov qab yug los ua neb leej ntxhais rau lub neej yav tom ntej.
(I pray that I can be reborn as your daughter once again, in the next life.)

Txuas ntxiv no mus, kuv yuav hais lus Mekas los piav txog kuv lub hom phiaj mus kawm ntawv.
(Furthermore, I will explain in English my inspirations for pursuing higher education.)

The number-one question I am always asked since graduating school is, "What do you do with a theater arts degree?" and I always smile because being a theater artist or artist in general, in this day and age, is difficult. I perform many different jobs and play many different roles because artists are often undervalued, underpaid, and discouraged, often told to "get a real job." But even more difficult than this is being a Hmong female artist.

A lot of you may not know this, but growing up in elementary school and middle school, I was your stereotypical shy, quiet Hmong girl. But on the inside, I always knew I had so much that I wanted to do and so much I wanted to say. However, no matter how much I wanted to be heard, I always silenced myself, for fear of rejection and judgment. I was never a studious child. The only reason I wanted to go to school was to see my friends. And the only thing I looked forward to was playing outside at recess, because my friends and I would play "Cinderella," and guess who was always Cinderella? Yup. Me. I always loved playing different characters and living in this dream world I built with my imagination. Overall, I disliked school because I didn't think it was going to be useful for my career . . . as the next Britney Spears. Funny thing was, I had all these aspirations to be a famous pop star, but would never let anyone hear me sing. It went on like this for years. I was convinced I'd be the next Mary-Kate and Ashley Olsen, but I refused to perform for people.

In middle school, that all changed for me, though. I joined choir to get out of study hall, and I remember it like it was yesterday. I came in late. The only seat left was in the first row, directly in front of the choir teacher. I sat down. She finished taking attendance, and we began warm-ups. I sang with the class, as she instructed, but before I could even blink, she told the room to be quiet. "Shh! Who was singing?" And I knew she was talking about me. A million thoughts began to haunt my mind. *Oh, no! I sang too loud. I am in such big trouble! Why did I think I could sing so loud?* I slowly raised my hand, on the verge of tears. She looked at me and asked for my name. "Hrm . . . Gaosong . . . what a beautiful name. You have a beautiful voice. Never stop singing, okay, Gaosong?" She continued teaching the class, and I played it cool, as if nothing happened. But on the inside, I couldn't understand why anyone would think my voice was beautiful. I couldn't understand why anyone would think my Hmong name was beautiful. I couldn't understand why anyone would associate beauty with me, a quiet, ugly, chubby Hmong girl. But I do know one thing: since that moment, I have never stopped singing. Because for the first time in my life, I found my voice. I wasn't ever going to let anyone or myself silence it again.

As I got into high school, my mother was worried that I was no longer speaking Hmong and I was losing my culture, so she made me take Hmong singing lessons. Little did my mother know, I purposefully chose not to speak Hmong and avoided Hmong people and Hmong culture because I secretly hated being Hmong. After six months of lessons, for our graduation the class entered the annual singing competition at the Hmong New Year Celebration in St. Paul. Before I knew it, the day of the competition had come. There I was, all dressed up in my Hmong clothes at the Hmong New Year. Thousands of people filled the Roy Wilkins Auditorium. I was next in the lineup, and petrified. The girl who thought she knew everything about singing, who said she was going to be the next Beyoncé, the girl who hated herself because she was Hmong was about to perform for thousands of Hmong people.

"I can't do it, Mom. I can't do it. I don't remember the words!" My mother was right by my side. She grabbed me, with tears in her eyes, and said, "No matter what happens today, I am so proud of you and I will always love you."

The audience clapped as the emcee announced my name. I

wiped away my tears and slowly stepped up onto the stage. The lights were bright, and the stage was large. The auditorium was packed; there wasn't an empty seat or any standing room on the ground level. I stood there, center stage, and smiled, like I had practiced a million times before. Silence filled the room for what felt like an eternity. When the music began, the audience screamed with joy before I even sang a single note. For the first time, I sang my heart out. At the end of the song, I bowed, and the audience got up on their feet and cheered for me. As I walked off the stage, I begin bawling. My mother was there to catch me as I floated in the air. I couldn't believe it: these Hmong people, the people I had hated so much, showed me so much love, kindness, and support. I vowed, in that moment, that I would never ever doubt my people again.

Fast-forward almost a decade since that performance. I was studying music performance in voice at the University of Minnesota. During that time in my life, I had completely forgotten what it meant to be a Hmong woman and a Hmong artist because I was so focused on trying to fit into the mold of a successful opera-singer-in-training. But as destiny would have it, studying opera no longer resonated with who I was in that moment in my life. So I transferred to the theater arts program, not knowing if it was the right decision or if it would help me become the artist I always wanted to be. That first semester in the program, I took a theater history course and found my calling. We learned that the origins of theater is not from Greece or Rome. It is from ritual, such as Hmong marriage rituals or funeral rites. In that moment, so many questions filled my mind about my people and my culture and about myself. I knew I made the right choice to study theater. Because I knew I would dedicate the rest of my life to studying and researching Hmong arts and Hmong performance practices.

Since graduating, I am proud to say that I have had my Hmong music and performances aired on Classical Minnesota Public Radio. I am proud to say that I have acted professionally all over the Twin Cities and Greater Minnesota, and I am honored to have written short creative nonfiction pieces and folktales for the Children's Theatre Company that are currently being taught in schools all over the metro area. But this path has not been easy. Oftentimes, many people, including Hmong people, think that art, theater, and performance are a waste of time. They think that when I make theater, I am playing around and not taking my life seriously. But I can promise you, when I go teach theater to a class of Southeast Asian refugee students, and I am the only adult person of color and the only Hmong artist in the room, these little kids do not think it is a waste of time. They feel so special, because for the first time they have a teacher who looks like them, who sounds like them, who knows the stories and struggles of their people, and they feel heard. They feel important. They feel loved for who they are as individuals. And for the first time, they feel like they can dare to dream their own impossible dreams.

Being a Hmong female artist is not an easy path, but most things worth having in life are not easy. It takes dedication, hard work, passion for your craft and for the people you are serving, but most of all, it takes the love and support of the people in your life. That's why I want to give thanks to my family. All of my accomplishments would not be possible without the love and support of my family and friends, but I especially want to say thank you to my fearless brothers and sisters. They have supported me, given me strength, and shown me that I am capable of anything. I have learned from their journeys, and now I am not afraid to forge my own path. I make art because it is a part of who I am and how I express myself. *Artist* is not my occupation. It is who I am. We are all artists; it's just whether or not that inner artist is nourished and given the opportunity to speak for itself.

Success, life, happiness—all seem like impossible dreams, but the most impossible dream is being able to find your true calling, staring it dead in the eye and accepting it for all of its wondrous fear and glory. And it's never-ending: as we continue to grow, so does this dream.

So, what do you do with a theater arts degree? This degree has given me the courage, different perspectives, and tools with which to navigate my impossible dream and to give light to the beautiful art, culture, and history of my people. A degree does not define your self-worth; it's the blood, sweat, and tears that go into any journey that truly define your character and potential for success and happiness in the future. May you always continue to strive to turn your impossible dreams into reality.

Gaosong V. Heu is a performance artist, musician, teaching artist, published writer, and scholar of Hmong performance practices.

Malia Yang-Xiong's Leadership with Hmong Students

Npaus Baim Her
Edited by Mailia Yang-Xiong

In the early 2000s, I was hired as a cultural liaison for the White Bear Lake Area Schools (WBLAS) district. I was the first Hmong staff person hired and one of very few hired staff of color. The Hmong population in the area was growing, and Hmong students made up the largest minority group in the schools. My position as a liaison allowed me to work with school staff and Hmong families. Many teachers at that time were unfamiliar with Hmong culture and its community. A majority of Hmong parents were first generation and either had limited English proficiency or needed support to navigate the school system.

I had the opportunity to reach out to Hmong students, too, and to do this, I reflected on my own experiences. As I grew up in a suburban area and attended predominantly white schools, there were no books made available to me that reflected on who I was as an Asian student. Books catering to white students, such as *Of Mice and Men* and *To Kill a Mockingbird*, were given as reading assignments. As I worked in the WBLAS, I didn't see many changes made in curriculums that reflected the needs and identities of students of color. I felt that for teachers to be able to connect with their students of color, they needed to dig deeper and provide materials that were relatable for students of different ethnicities. As a liaison, I could only provide materials or make suggestions; the teachers were the ones who controlled the decisions that impacted changes to the learning materials they provided students.

When I discovered the book *Hey, Hmong Girl, Whassup?: The Journal of Choua Vang* by Leah Rempel (2004), I wanted to provide a way to share it with Hmong students immediately. I was excited that the main character in this book was a Hmong girl. How often do you find that in a book? I started a Hmong Girls Reading Circle in one of the middle schools. We met once a week during the students' homeroom hour that was normally when they were required to read silently on their own.

I asked, "Why have the students read in silence when we could read together?" The reading circle was an opportunity to connect with Hmong students while creating a safe space where students could gather to read, discuss, and develop their own voices. During that time, none of the schools had extracurricular programs that focused on Hmong students. Most Hmong girls were expected to return home after school to watch their younger siblings. Participation in school activities was not recommended by their parents. Sharing reading material that was different from the usual school materials was a way to expose Hmong girls to possibilities.

Not all Hmong girls in that middle school participated in the reading circle. My choice to focus on Hmong girls was based on my own years as a teenager. There were different expectations for Hmong girls than Hmong boys. I wanted the Hmong girls to dream beyond the path of early marriage. With my generation, a lot of the girls were brought up to think that it was more important to be an obedient Hmong wife than to have a higher education. By age sixteen or seventeen, girls were considered old maids. I once met a girl who told me, "I want to get married because if I wait too long, I will be too old and no one will want me." I thought, *Wait a second. We're both only sixteen!* Since I wasn't getting these same messages at home, I said, "I'm not old! What are you talking about?!" I didn't want to get married. I was very fortunate that my mother told me to focus on school because she didn't want me to have a job that doesn't pay well. Because of my mom's lack of education and limited English, she worked as a housekeeper. She often talked about how exhausting the work was since it was all manual labor. I was a petite girl, so she told me that manual work would be hard on my back. I'm glad she encouraged me to pursue higher education so that I could have a different lifestyle. I channeled my mother's energy into the Hmong girls and encouraged them to take on leadership roles so that they could determine their own future. When our Hmong girls are empowered, they can strive to be anything. They are resilient and strong.

During my years with the WBLAS, I advised many after-school programs, such as Hmong Women's Circle, Journey, Hmong Heritage Club, and Culture Club, also known for some years as Koom Siab. I also oversaw the program Hmong Men's Circle. Although these programs differ by name, their objectives were similar in that the programs supported students to develop team-building and leadership skills and explored postsecondary education and college visits. I hadn't discovered the endless possibility of opportunities until I was in college, so when I worked in the schools, I wanted our next Hmong generation to dream early about who they could become. Since I had the means to access opportunities for the next generation to discover their possibilities, I felt it was my responsibility to share this knowledge with them. Wherever I was able to minimize the challenges and obstacles that stood in the way of Hmong students getting to where they wanted to go, I did so. When doors of opportunities were open to students, I saw the light in them, the young leaders, ignite.

Culture Club was the program that ran the longest. It was different from my other programs because it had a student board. Students were elected to the board so they could have firsthand experiences with leadership. As board members, they jointly led the student club members. They had to learn to work together even though each of them had different leadership styles. There were times when the student board spoke about the difficulties in leading student members and the challenges they encountered in getting student members to participate. The challenge for them as young leaders was to find a middle ground between them and the members so that club gatherings were positive experiences for all. Some student leaders reported that they were able to apply the leadership skills they learned in the club toward their college and personal experiences.

I believe that when you work with youth, it is important to help them understand their leadership styles. When they understand their strength as leaders, then they can lead and support others. Since we are all different people, different leadership styles are needed to meet different personalities. Student leaders learned quickly that club members have different personalities. Some members are quiet, some are outgoing, some dependent, some independent, some calm, some loud, and the list goes on. Student leaders had to set their differences aside and learn to work together. Leadership comes in many ways and forms. They lead, make mistakes, and learn to grow from their mistakes. They lead without bias, without fear, with courage, with determination, and they inspire others.

I reached out to Hmong students in different ways. I tried not to force anyone into an uncomfortable situation. I avoided creating spaces that would push anyone away. In the Hmong Girls Reading Circle, I knew that some students were shy, so I showed respect and celebrated their attendance. When the reading circle was not the place to connect with the shy students, I approached them with a one-to-one meeting. I connected with students by reaching out to them at their comfort level. When the students reached back, that indicated I could then challenge them with more. By knowing the students' interests, I was able to introduce them to opportunities that allowed them to explore new experiences. When we discover our passion, it is that passion that will drive and push us to do the things that we do. We come together, work together, and learn together.

Npaus Baim Her is furthering her education through University of Minnesota Duluth's English master's program and has been given the opportunity to teach college writing as a graduate instructor. She serves as secretary on the board of directors for a nonprofit organization, Minors, and also volunteers as a writing assistant, collecting Secret War stories for the organization's book project to educate Hmong youth about their elders' history. She has exhibited her art and literary work with HECUA (Higher Education Consortium for Urban Affairs) Alumni, Prior Affairs, and the Coalition of Asian American Leaders.

History of Hnub Tshiab

Hnub Tshiab works to develop Hmong women leaders to be "a catalyst for lasting cultural, institutional and social change to improve the lives of Hmong women."

Mission

Hnub Tshiab: Hmong Women Achieving Together began in 1998 at the Wilder Foundation as a grassroots volunteer group to address violence against women in the Hmong community and became its own nonprofit in 2010. Its original name was the Hmong Women's Action Team. The community initiative that formed Hnub Tshiab was called Hmoob Thaj Yeeb (Hmong Peace), or the Hmong Violence Prevention Initiative. It began as a community organizing and mobilization effort to engage members of the Hmong community, nonprofits, and public agencies to prevent violence and design services to support the Hmong community. Hmoob Thaj Yeeb affiliated with the Initiative for Violence-Free Families and Communities in Ramsey County for systems change. In the planning process, more than a thousand community members were engaged, and they identified that sexism was a root cause of violence against Hmong women and girls. This formed the original mission of Hnub Tshiab, which was to "end violence against Hmong women by ending sexism." In 2008, Hnub Tshiab incorporated as a nonprofit organization with the mission *to be a catalyst for lasting cultural, institutional and social change to improve the lives of Hmong women,* demonstrating organizational growth by reconceptualizing the solution to the social issue of women's inequality. Instead of *fighting sexism,* Hnub Tshiab focused on *empowering women* (a different means to the same goal).

Hnub Tshiab: Hmong Women Achieving Together is an organization for Hmong women, led by Hmong women. We empower
Hmong women by developing their leadership and by engaging
families and communities in building insight and understanding
about the changing dynamics of Hmong culture. We ask people
to question social constructs around gender and gain insight
around how social constructs impact our daily lives. Social constructs were built by humans; humans therefore have the power
to deconstruct them. We assert that it is okay for Hmong women
to focus on Hmong women and it is okay to talk about sexism
and gender inequality in our endeavor to promote Hmong wom-
en's autonomy and leadership.

Vision

We envision a world where Hmong women and girls are valued
and supported to achieve their highest potential in all of their
roles. We see a society that honors the choices that Hmong
women make and celebrates their ability to direct their own
destinies.

Change Framework

At Hnub Tshiab, we believe there must first be awareness and
acknowledgment that gender, as a social construct, is a powerful
force that shapes the lives of members of the entire community.
By focusing on understanding ourselves, our families, our culture, and our community, we can begin to reflect on and start
the systemic change necessary to improve the lives of Hmong
women and girls. We create knowledge through dialogue, reflection, and self-study. We provide leadership and advocacy to build
coalitions and community focused on social change to improve
the lives of those around us. By starting with a shared vision of a
better world for Hmong women and girls, coalitions for change
can occur to inspire, leverage, and ensure equity. The change
framework is linked to the belief that we have the power to create and strengthen our own community.

Hnub Tshiab's Beginnings

Hnub Tshiab: Hmong Women Achieving Together is about empowering Hmong women. We have gone through a twenty-year journey in our understanding of empowerment. Some argue that because of exposure to Western notions of feminism and women's equality, Hmong women now impose these Western ideals onto our own culture, causing it to be judged and pathologized. However, many of our mothers will argue that they have always realized their positions of powerlessness and wished to have the same rights as men; they just never had the option to do anything about it. Now that we are in the United States, we have legal rights to support us to utilize our agency, take action, and harness our own internal power. We didn't need Western culture to teach us about women's lack of equality—we were already aware of it—but we did need to be in a land that allowed us to exercise our basic human rights: the right to equality and autonomy and the freedom to speak up. We are not pathologizing our own culture; we wish to change the parts that are no longer helpful to a majority of its members and empower those who have lacked power for so long.

Empowerment is a process of moving from a position of powerlessness to mobilization, where one is able to take action to create change in one's life.[1]

Empowerment begins with a realization of one's own position of powerlessness. Hnub Tshiab started in 1998 as the Hmong Women's Action Team, a group formed under the umbrella of Ramsey County Initiative for Violence-Free Families. During this

---

1. Here and below: Lorraine M. Gutiérrez, "Working with Women of Color: An Empowerment Perspective," *Social Work* 35, no. 2 (1990): 149–53; Carr E. Summerson, "Rethinking Empowerment Theory Using a Feminist Lens: The Importance of Process," *Affilia* 18, no. 8 (2003): 8–20.

time, Hmong women identified concerns they faced, most notably the need to end domestic violence against Hmong women
and girls. Hmong women had already realized their powerlessness within Hmong culture, and we knew the forces behind this
powerlessness.

Following the next stage of empowerment, we began to critically analyze our own predicament, including the beliefs that
are passed down to us, rather than accepting the status quo.
The Hmong Women's Action Team put new words to Hmong
women's status. Hmong women were too afraid to share their
experiences publicly, fearing the tigerbite. In 1998, the results of a
survey of thousands of Hmong community members were documented in a report titled, "Taking a Public Stand: Completing
the Journey from War to Peace: Through the Ending of Violence:
A Community Action Plan to Prevent Violence in the Hmong
Community." The findings extrapolated cultural practices that
result in the devaluing of Hmong women and support a power
imbalance that perpetuates women's lower status in Hmong society. The findings of this report included:

First, daughters and sons are treated differently. There is a
general lack of respect for females and a lack of support for
daughters because they will marry out of the clan. Often our
community stays silent about sons or males who actively mal-
treat or degrade females.

Second, educated wives are not valued, and their contributions go unrecognized. Educated, older wives are seen as un-
controllable and too independent. Young, teenage wives who
are more vulnerable and easier to control are sometimes valued
more.

Third, marriage is valued above physical and emotional safety
in an abusive relationship. There is little support and few resources for Hmong women who want to get out of an abusive
relationship. Few men and women believe a husband is guilty for
hitting his wife. A woman is usually stigmatized if she leaves an
abusive marriage. Being divorced is worse than being a widow or
a second wife because of the value of marriage. As a widow or a
divorcée, a woman has no social status in the Hmong community because she is not associated with a man.

Fourth, having many children is valued above the reproductive health or rights of women. In some families, the woman does not have control of her own reproduction. Often, having many children is a result of her powerlessness or her ambivalence in controlling unwanted pregnancies in the face of pressure to have more children.

Fifth, males are believed to be born with more power than females. Families tend to reinforce through parenting that girls are weaker and should be subservient to men. Women often blame themselves, believing they deserve punishment when abused. Men learn it is their right to expect obedience from women.

And finally, marriage structures set the stage for violence. Large age differences between husbands and wives, such as men who are in their thirties or forties marrying teenagers, sets up a power dynamic that may lead to violence.

Teens forced to marry because of a pregnancy or to save face are cut off from many opportunities. Family violence may result from community tolerance of second/minor wives and women marrying men who are already married. According to some participants, early marriage is a form of violence against women, especially if the bride is young and forced into the relationship. Marrying young and birthing children early limits her opportunities for social, emotional, and economic growth.

Based on these findings, the Hmong Women's Action Team was created with the mission *to end violence against Hmong women and girls by ending sexism*. This mission was revised in 2007: *to be a catalyst for lasting cultural, institutional and social change to improve the lives of Hmong women.* By raising awareness of their own predicament and their own self-empowerment work, the women of the Hmong Women's Action Team took ownership of the language used to describe their own predicaments and conceptualized the solution as one that focused on *empowering the women rather than tackling the sexism.* Again, this framework represented a different means to the same goal.

The third stage of empowerment is to develop a group consciousness. We needed to raise awareness and bring more women into this new awareness. We did this through one of our first newsletters, *Hnub Tshiab* (A New Day; pronounced: *Hnoo Chia*), which we distributed throughout the Twin Cities. Other efforts to raise awareness included speaking at conferences and collaborating with mainstream groups such as the Women's Consortium and the Minnesota Coalition for Battered Women.

These awareness-raising efforts helped to form a group consciousness among Hmong women, leading to the final stage of empowerment, which is mobilization. In this stage, the oppressed organize and prepare to take action in order to create change within their own lives. Mobilization came in the form of increasing women's status within the community. Hmong Women Achieving Together convened a second group of Hmong women in 2005 in Sandstone, Minnesota, where we identified that the same issues (sexism, violence, etc.) continued to plague Hmong women. Following this retreat, Hnub Tshiab chose to move the organization to a new level, incorporating with our new mission in 2007. We envision a world where Hmong women and girls are valued and supported to achieve their highest potential in all their roles.

We are no longer just victims of patriarchy and sexism; instead, we have inherent power simply because we are autonomous humans, and we can create change within the social systems to which we, too, belong. We have a role in these systems, as do men. We CAN create change to improve our own lives in partnership with men, our families, and our community. We can't empower others if we are unable to enact our own sense of agency. We must be able to harness our self-power as an inherent part of this work. We are BEING empowered as we are DOING empowerment.

We are empowering Hmong women by developing leaders. In 2008, we created the Hmong Women Leadership Institute, from which graduated our ninth cohort (a total of 108 women) in 2019. Our Hmong Girls Leadership Training Institute was launched in 2017 and graduated in its first cohort twenty Hmong girls who will continue the work of Hnub Tshiab. We also recognize Hmong women leaders through our Hmong Woman of the Year award and provide leadership training through our board. We reach out to Hmong families and men through the Intergenerational Retreat and Family Dialogues, and we collaborate with several community entities to further our work. We increased and maintained our network of Hmong women through our breakfast series with the graduates of the Hmong Women Leadership Institute as well as through outreach and collaboration with other organizations.

Our next goal is to build a space for Hmong women. We envision a house, a safe space where Hmong women can gather, in the spirit of the settlement houses that American women created for other women in our early history. These settlement houses became community centers that still exist today.

Hnub Tshiab Board Members

Pa Der Vang (2000–Present)
Dr. Pa Der Vang is an associate professor at St. Catherine University/University of St. Thomas School of Social Work, coordinator of the critical Hmong studies minor at St. Catherine University, and a cofounder of Hnub Tshiab. She received her master's degree and PhD in social work from the University of Minnesota Twin Cities. She practiced as a clinical social worker for eight years before starting her teaching career. She has published articles on the effect of teenage marriage on Hmong women and cultural change among Hmong in America. Her current research is on Hmong Americans and the effects of acculturation.

Kao Ly Ilean Her (2007–Present)
Kao Ly Ilean Her is the chief executive officer of the Hmong Elders Center, an adult day center serving Hmong seniors in the St. Paul/Minneapolis area. As executive director of the Council on Asian-Pacific Minnesotans, Kao Ly was at the forefront of establishing legislation, policy, and programs to address the community's critical needs. She has founded the nonprofits Allies for Mentoring Asian Youth, Hnub Tshiab: Hmong Women Achieving Together, and the Heritage Center for Asian Americans and Pacific Islanders and served as a trustee of the Minneapolis Foundation, the Asian Pacific Endowment of the St. Paul Foundation, and Women's Foundation of Minnesota.

Cindi Yang (2015–Present)
Cindi Yang oversees child care assistance, child development services, and the Office of Economic Opportunity at Minnesota's Department of Human Services. She leads work to promote the well-being of children and self-sufficiency of families. Cindi

served as director of programs and public policy at Neighborhood House, whose programs help stabilize the lives of families
and break the cycle of poverty. Cindi was a community faculty
professor at Metropolitan State University's department of social
work. She cofounded the Minnesota Hmong Social Work Coalition, creating a space to develop Hmong social workers as leaders
in their field.

Gao Thor (2015–Present)

Gao Thor, a psychology major and educational studies/religious
studies minor at Macalester College, is the capacity associate
for the Amherst H. Wilder Foundation's Youth Leadership Initiative, a multicultural program that provides young people the
opportunity to build skills and qualities needed to be agents of
change. She has more than five years of experience in tackling
community issues through youth leadership development, facili-
tating dialogues around personal narratives, and facilitation
training. Gao received a Davis Projects for Peace $10,000 grant
to design and facilitate a program with young Hmong women
about personal narratives to address gender equity in the Hmong
community.

Leona Thao (2016–Present)

Leona Thao is an evaluation specialist with Minneapolis Public Schools, supporting the district's equity framework and ensuring that it has equitable policies, practices, procedures, and
budgets. Leona brings not only her passion for gender and racial
justice but experiences in evaluation and public policy to the
Hnub Tshiab board. She graduated from Hnub Tshiab's Hmong
Women Leadership Institute Program in 2014. Leona earned
a bachelor's degree in business management from the Spears
School of Business at Oklahoma State University and a master's
in public policy from the Hubert H. Humphrey School of Public
Affairs at the University of Minnesota.

Ma Xiong (2017–Present)

Ma Xiong is a corporate compliance associate analyst with Allianz
Life Insurance Company. She is passionate about empowering

girls of color to lead their own lives and contribute to the success of their communities. Ma received her law degree from Mitchell Hamline School of Law and her bachelor's degree from the University of St. Thomas with majors in entrepreneurship and legal studies in business. She has experience in the nonprofit, legal, and corporate sectors.

Chee Lor (2017–Present)
Chee Lor was born in Ban Vinai refugee camp in Thailand, was raised in St. Paul, Minnesota, and earned her master's in social work at the University of Minnesota Twin Cities. She is passionate about empowering Hmong girls and women to be the leaders they want to see and enabling them to be their most authentic selves in reaching for their dreams. She is an alumna of Hnub Tshiab's Hmong Women Leadership Institute and has found her calling in doing work that supports and lifts Hmong girls and women much like herself.

Yer Lor (2017–Present)
Yer Lor was born and raised on the east side of St. Paul and has a degree in political science and Spanish studies with a minor in leadership from the University of Minnesota Twin Cities. She is director of community partnership for Girl Scouts of Minnesota and Wisconsin River Valleys, overseeing their ConnectZ program, which provides the Girl Scout experience to girls who often face access barriers. She also worked at Neighborhood House as a program facilitator and at United Family for All Families as a youth organizer. Yer is an alumna of Hnub Tshiab's Hmong Women Leadership Institute.

Reading Guide

The tiger is considered a mystical character, eliciting wonder, mystery, and awe in Hmong culture. The tiger is feared and respected for its strength and prowess, yet the tiger is vulnerable, as it has been outwitted by humans in Hmong folktales. Although the tiger is considered a quiet, solitary animal, in folklore it is often portrayed interacting with Hmong in very complex ways.

Hmong believe the tiger should not be approached; that is why in folklore, when Hmong are depicted interacting with the tiger, there is often a sense of fear, ambivalence, courage, awe, mystery, and danger. The term *tigerbite* (tsov tom), often considered a slur in Hmong culture, is used to refer to individuals to indicate lack of foresight, impulsiveness, malice, and lack of intelligence. Someone who is a tsov tom would actually approach a tiger—and get bitten.

1. Why would staring down the tiger elicit the accusation that one is a tsov tom (impulsive, lacking foresight, lacking intelligence)?

2. How do individuals challenge this notion that to stare down the tiger is to lack intelligence? What might staring down the tiger imply of a person's character, capacity, resilience, strength, and resources?

3. *Staring down the tiger* may be a metaphor for taking on risks, challenging norms, or pushing boundaries. Under what circumstances might someone choose to challenge social norms and push social boundaries?

4. How do the women in the stories in *Staring Down the Tiger* challenge their prescribed roles as wife, mother, daughter, Hmong woman?

5. Because Hmong culture is interdependent and collectivist, it is often frowned upon to speak about one's successes. Why should these stories be told, and what can we learn from them? What do we lose if we do not make room for these stories to be told?

6. How do the stories collected here inform our communities? What impact might these stories have on individuals who read them?

7. How else can we interpret a Hmong woman's choice to stare down the tiger?

8. In what other ways do Hmong women stare down the tiger?

9. In what ways do women from other cultures stare down the tiger?

10. How do you stare down the tiger in your own life?

11. What might be some consequences of staring down the tiger at the individual level? Consider personal factors such as emotional consequences, psychological consequences, or loss of opportunity.

12. How might a woman risk harm to or loss of relationships by staring down the tiger? What are the competing pressures for women to conform, and what risks do women take by pushing social and cultural boundaries that seek to inhibit them?

13. What other situations could the metaphor of *staring down the tiger* represent?